Survey of Law School Faculty 2025, Use of AI Features from Major Legal Publishers

ISBN 979-8-88517-292-9

Table of contents

THE QUESTIONNAIRE

1. Please give us the following contact information:

   A. Name:
   B. Organization:
   C. Title
   D. Email address:
   E.

2. You are:

   A. Professor
   B. Assistant/Associate Professor
   C. Lecturer or Research Fellow
   D. Adjunct/Clinical Faculty
   E. Emeritus
   F. Other (please specify)

3. How old are you?

   A. Under 30
   B. 30-39
   C. 40-49
   D. 50-59
   E. 60 or Over

4. Are you male or female?

   A. Male
   B. Female
   C. Transgender

5. Your law school has approximately how many students?

6. Is your law school public or private?

   A. Public
   B. Private

7. In the past semester how many courses did you teach?

   A. None
   B. One
   C. Two
   D. More than Two

8. Which phrase best approximates the view of your law school taken by organizations that rank law schools?

A. Top 20 law school
B. Somewhere in the 21-75 rank
C. 76 to 250
D. Other

9. Which phrase best characterizes your political beliefs?

A. Right of Conservative
B. Conservative
C. Centrist
D. Liberal
E. Left of Liberal
F. Curriculum Development

10. How often do you use each of the following AI tools from major legal publishers?

	Not at all	Less than once a month	Monthly	Weekly	Daily	Several times a week
Lexis Brief Analyzer						
Westlaw Edge						
CoCounsel						
Lexis+						
Bloomberg Draft Analyzer						
Fastcase						
LawGeex						
EverLaw						
Luminance						
DoNotPay						

11. If you use Westlaw Edge, rate the usefulness to you of the following features

	Essential	Highly Useful	Often Useful	Sometimes Useful	Not really Useful	Not really familiar with this feature
Westlaw Answers						
Litigation Analytics						
WestSearch Plus						
Statutes or Regulations Compare						
KeyCite Overruling Risk						
Brief Analysis						
Contract Review						

12. If you use Lexis+, rate the usefulness to you of the following features:

	Essential	Highly Useful	Often Useful	Sometimes Useful	Not really Useful	Not really familiar with this feature
Les Machina						
Judicial Analytics						
Shephard's Enhanced Analytics						
Research Map						
Content Recommendations						
Brief Analyzer						
Contract Review						

13. How important do you feel that it is to equip law students with the skills to use the newest emerging artificial intelligence powered legal research tools of legal publishers and information services?

A. Extremely important
B. Very important
C. Somewhat important
D. Not so important
E. Not at all important

14. How helpful has your law school library been in explaining how to use these new tools?

A. Extremely helpful
B. Very helpful
C. Somewhat helpful
D. Not so helpful
E. Not at all helpful

Characteristics of the sample

Academic title

	#
Professor	61
Assistant/Associate Professor	21
Adjunct/Clinical Faculty	28
Emeritus	15
Other	9
Total	134

Age of respondent

	#
Under 40	6
40-49	19
50-59	33
60 or over	75
Unknown	1
Total	134

Gender of respondent

	#
Male	80
Female	50
Other	4
Total	134

Public or private law school

	#
Public	81
Private	53
Total	134

# of courses taught las semester

	#

None	27
One	40
Two	59
More than two	8
Total	134

Ranking

	#
Top 20 law school	27
Somewhere in the 21-75 rank	55
76 to 250	46
Other	6
Total	134

Political views

	#
Conservative	14
Centrist	34
Liberal	65
Left of Liberal	20
Unknown	1
Total	134

Law school enrollment

	#
Less than 400	32
400+ - 550	32
550+ - 800	34
More than 800	36
Total	134

INSTITUTIONAL AFFILIATIONS OF THE SURVEY PARTICIPANTS

IU McKinney
Belmont University College of Law
Benjamin N. Cardozo School of Law
Bennett Law Firm
Boston University School of Law
BU School of Law
Buffalo State University
Cardozo
Carey Law, U Maryland
Charleston School of Law
Chicago-Kent
Columbia Law School
Creighton University School of Law
Duke Law
Emory University
FisherBroyles
Fordham University School of Law
Harvard Law School
Howard University
Indiana University
LMU Loyola Law School
Louisiana State Univ. Law Center
LSU Law Center Juvenile Defense Clinic
LSU Law, Tulane law
Marquette University Law School
MC Law
McGill University
Mercer Univ. School of Law
Mississippi Supreme Court
Mitchell Hamline School of Law
MSU College of Law
New England Law | Boston
Northeastern University School of Law
Northern Illinois University College of Law
Northwestern Law School

OU Law
Pace Law School
Pepperdine Caruso Law
Public Counsel
Roger Williams University School of Law
Rutgers Law School
Salesforce, Inc.
Santa Clara University School of Law
Schulich School of Law
SMU Law School
Southern University Law Center
St. Mary's University School of Law
Stetson University College of Law
Temple Law School
The Ohio State University Moritz College of Law
The University of Tennessee College of Law
Thomas Jefferson School of Law
Thurgood Marshall S of Law
UCI law
UCLA School of Law
UGA School of Law
UIC Law
UMass Law School
UMKC Law School
UNC-CH
Univ. of Washington School of Law
University of Arkansas
University of California Irvine Law School
University of California San Francisco Law School
University of Connecticut Law School
University of Florida
University of Georgia Law School
University of Idaho
University of Illinois Chicago Law School
University of Iowa, College of Law
University of Maryland School of Law
University of Mississippi, School of Law
University of Nebraska - Lincoln College of Law
University of North Carolina School of Law
University of Oklahoma College of Law
University of Oregon School of Law
University of Richmond
University of South Dakota Law School
University of St. Thomas -- Minnesota
University of Tennessee
University of Texas
University of Toronto
University of Tulsa

University of Virginia
University of Wyoming
UT Law and Bush School
UVA Law
UW School of Law
Villanova University
Washington Univ in St Louis
Wayne State University Law School
William S. Boyd School of Law, UNLV
Wise Law Library, CU Boulder
Yale Law School

SUMMARY OF MAIN FINDINGS

This survey provides insights into the usage patterns of AI tools from major legal publishers by law faculty, broken down by various demographic and institutional variables.

Lexis Brief Analyzer Usage

- Overall Usage: 79.10% of law faculty reported using the Lexis Brief Analyzer "Not at all," with only 3.73% using it at least monthly and 5.22%, less than once a month.

- By Law School Enrollment: Smaller law schools (fewer than 400 students) had the highest usage rate, with 84.38% using it "Not at all."

- By Academic Title: Professors (83.61%) were the least likely to use this tool, with most usage being sporadic (monthly or less).

- By Age: Younger faculty under 40 were more likely to use it, with 16.67% using it monthly, though still the majority (66.67%) did not use it at all.

- By Gender: Male and female faculty had similar high non-usage rates (77.50% and 80.00%, respectively).

- By Law School Type: Faculty at private law schools used it less frequently (84.91% "Not at all") compared to those at public law schools (75.31% "Not at all").

Westlaw Edge Usage

- Overall Usage: 48.51% reported not using Westlaw Edge at all, but there was a more even spread among those who used it monthly (9.70%) to weekly (8.96%).

- By Law School Enrollment: Faculty at larger schools (more than 800 students) used the tool more frequently, with 16.67% using it at least monthly.

- By Academic Title: Assistant/Associate Professors showed the highest usage rates overall with more than 38% using this tool at least monthly and 14.29% using it several times per week.

- By Age: Middle aged respondents (50-59) showed the most frequent use, with 18.18% using it weekly.

- By Gender: More female faculty (12.00%) used Westlaw Edge weekly compared to male faculty (7.50%). Also, 6% of female faculty used it daily while no male respondents used it daily. In general, use was much higher among females than males.

-By Law School Ranking: Use was quite modest among those at top 20 law schools and monthly, weekly and daily use rates were much higher among faculty at lower ranked law schools.

CoCounsel Usage

- Overall Usage: A significant 79.85% of faculty reported not using CoCounsel at all, with minimal usage across other categories. Only about 7% of faculty used CoCounsel to any degree.

- By Law School Enrollment: Smaller schools (less than 400 students) reported the least use, with 81.25% "Not at all" using it.

- By Academic Title: Professors (83.61%) and Emeritus faculty (73.33%) had the highest "Not at all" usage rates. Use was by far the highest among assistant and associate professors who accounted for all use more common than monthly, and much of monthly use as well.

- By Age: Faculty aged 50-59 were most likely to use it monthly or more frequently. (6.06%).

- By Gender: Male faculty (77.50%) had higher non-usage rates compared to female faculty (82.00%). Almost all regular use in the sample was from female faculty.

- By Law School Type: Usage was slightly higher among faculty from public law schools (75.31% "Not at all") compared to private law schools (86.79%).

Lexis+ Usage

-Overall Use was fairly extensive with about 25% showing some use and more than 5% using Lexis+ at least weekly.

-By Academic Title: Sustained use of weekly or more was most common among full professors but occasional use was by far most popular among assistant/associate professors.

-By Age: Occasional use was most common among faculty under age 40 while sustained use was most common among those aged 40-59.

Bloomberg Draft Analyzer Usage

- Overall Usage: 83.58% of respondents indicated they never used Bloomberg Draft Analyzer, showing very low usage across the sample.

Fastcase Usage

- Overall Usage: Similar to other tools, Fastcase saw very limited use, with 76.12% of respondents not using it at all. About 3.75% of respondents were using Fastcase monthly or more commonly.

- By Academic Title: Professors had higher non-usage rates at 83.61%, with minimal use across other categories. Adjunct and clinical faculty accounted for most use and all use more common than monthly use.

- By Age: Non-usage was prevalent among all age groups, with faculty aged 50-59 using it the most (6.06% weekly).

- By Law School Type: Public law schools had higher usage overall, with 3.7% using it weekly or more commonly compared to 0.00% at private law schools.

Use of LawGeex

Overall Use: Only a small percentage – 1.49% -- have used LawGeex. All use was by private school law faculty, generally adjuncts.

Use of EverLaw

Overall Use: Use was modest – only 1.5% have ever used it. Most use was by adjunct faculty; all use was accounted for by female faculty.

Luminance Usage

- Overall Usage: No use was recorded in the sample.

DoNotPay Usage

- Overall Usage: Similar to other AI tools, the DoNotPay AI tool had low usage, with 82.84% of faculty never using it. Oly 1.49% had ever used it. All use in the sample was

AI Tool Feature Usefulness (Westlaw Edge-Specific)

- Westlaw Answers and Litigation Analytics were the least well-known features, with around 30-35% of respondents unfamiliar with them. Those not answering the question usually do not use the product family in question so have so opinion.
- WestSearch Plus and KeyCite Overruling Risk were the most used features, with moderate ratings of "Essential" or "Highly Useful."
- Statutes/Regulations Compare was also widely used, particularly in public law schools.
- Younger faculty and private law school faculty rated AI features as more useful than older faculty and public law school respondents.
- Usage of AI features correlated with the number of courses taught, with those teaching 1-2 courses more likely to engage with these tools.

Key Takeaways

1. Lexis Brief Analyzer, CoCounsel, and Bloomberg Draft Analyzer dominate AI tool usage in legal academia.
2. Westlaw Edge and its features are widely used, but there is a significant portion of faculty unfamiliar with its analytics and comparison tools.
3. Law faculty under 50, teaching 1-2 courses, and at private institutions are the most engaged with AI tools.
4. Smaller law schools have the highest engagement with AI tools, likely due to resource constraints requiring efficiency tools.
5. AI engagement is significantly lower among older faculty, conservative respondents, and faculty at top 20 law schools.

Lexis+ Feature Usefulness and AI Legal Research Education in Law Schools

Usefulness of Lexis+ Features

Survey respondents evaluated multiple Lexis+ features based on their usefulness. Across all features, a high proportion of respondents did not provide an answer (over 60%) or indicated that they were unfamiliar with the feature (ranging from 20% to 40%). Essential and highly useful ratings were relatively low, while a small percentage found some features “sometimes useful” or “often useful.”

Insights on Specific Features of Lexis+

- Les Machina & Judicial Analytics: More than 60% of respondents did not answer. Around 30%–40% were unfamiliar with these features. A small percentage – about 3.5% -- found them "often" or "sometimes" useful.
- Shephard’s Enhanced Analytics: Among the most recognized tools but still underutilized by most faculty. About 9% found it “highly”, “often” or “sometimes” useful.

- Research Map, Content Recommendations, Brief Analyzer, Contract Review: These features followed the same pattern of limited familiarity and usage but with small minorities finding them useful, sometimes highly so.

Assessment of Importance of AI Legal Research Education

- Nearly 30% of respondents consider it "extremely important" to equip law students with AI-powered legal research tools.
- A combined 63% of respondents rated it either "extremely" or "very important", indicating strong support.
- Only a small fraction (around 4%) believe it is "not so important" or "not at all important."

Breakdown by Demographics

- Younger faculty members (under 40) were the most supportive, with 50% rating AI training as "extremely important."
- Female faculty were more likely (36%) than male faculty (22%) to rate AI training as extremely important.
- Faculty at lower-ranked law schools (76-250) were the most likely to see AI education as very important (41%).
- Liberal respondents showed the strongest support (40% rated it "very important").

Evaluation of Helpfulness of Law School Libraries in AI Training

- Only 16% of respondents found their law school library "extremely helpful", while 23% found them "very helpful" in equipping students to use the new IA features of major legal publishers.
- However, over 25% said libraries were only "somewhat helpful," and another 20% found them "not so" or "not at all helpful."
- Assistant/associate professors had the most positive views on library assistance.
- Smaller law schools (<400 students) and top 20 law schools were the least likely to find their libraries helpful.
- Younger faculty (under 40) were the most satisfied, while older faculty were more skeptical about library support.

Key Takeaways

1. Low Engagement with Lexis+ AI Features – Most respondents were either unfamiliar with or did not use Lexis+ features, highlighting a potential gap in AI training and awareness.
2. Strong Support for AI Legal Research Training – The majority agree that law students should be trained in emerging AI-powered tools, but faculty adoption remains low.

3. Law School Libraries Need Improvement – While some find library instruction useful, many believe more effort is needed to support AI research tool training.
4. Generational & Institutional Differences – Younger faculty and lower-ranked law schools are more open to AI legal tools, while senior faculty and top-tier law schools show lower engagement.

Table 1 How often do you use each of the following AI tools from major legal publishers?

Table 1.1.1 How often do you use each of the following AI tools from major legal publishers? Lexis Brief Analyzer.

	No Answer	Not at all	Less than once a month	Monthly	Weekly	Several times a week	Daily
Entire sample	11.94%	79.10%	5.22%	1.49%	1.49%	0.75%	0.00%

Table 1.1.2 How often do you use each of the following AI tools from major legal publishers? Lexis Brief Analyzer. Broken out by law school enrollment

Law school enrollment	No Answer	Not at all	Less than once a month	Monthly	Weekly	Several times a week	Daily
Less than 400	12.50%	84.38%	3.13%	0.00%	0.00%	0.00%	0.00%
400+ - 550	9.38%	75.00%	9.38%	3.13%	3.13%	0.00%	0.00%
550+ - 800	8.82%	82.35%	8.82%	0.00%	0.00%	0.00%	0.00%
More than 800	16.67%	75.00%	0.00%	2.78%	2.78%	2.78%	0.00%

Table 1.1.3 How often do you use each of the following AI tools from major legal publishers? Lexis Brief Analyzer. Broken out by academic title

Academic title	No Answer	Not at all	Less than once a month	Monthly	Weekly	Several times a week	Daily
Professor	13.11%	83.61%	0.00%	1.64%	1.64%	0.00%	0.00%
Assistant/ Associate Professor	9.52%	76.19%	9.52%	0.00%	0.00%	4.76%	0.00%
Adjunct/ Clinical Faculty	7.14%	78.57%	10.71%	0.00%	3.57%	0.00%	0.00%
Emeritus	20.00%	73.33%	6.67%	0.00%	0.00%	0.00%	0.00%
Other	11.11%	66.67%	11.11%	11.11%	0.00%	0.00%	0.00%

Table 1.1.4 How often do you use each of the following AI tools from major legal publishers? Lexis Brief Analyzer. Broken out by age of respondent

Age of respondent	No Answer	Not at all	Less than once a month	Monthly	Weekly	Several times a week	Daily
Under 40	16.67%	66.67%	16.67%	0.00%	0.00%	0.00%	0.00%
40-49	15.79%	73.68%	5.26%	5.26%	0.00%	0.00%	0.00%
50-59	6.06%	84.85%	6.06%	0.00%	0.00%	3.03%	0.00%
60 or over	13.33%	78.67%	4.00%	1.33%	2.67%	0.00%	0.00%
Unknown	0.00%	100.00%	0.00%	0.00%	0.00%	0.00%	0.00%

Table 1.1.5 How often do you use each of the following AI tools from major legal publishers? Lexis Brief Analyzer. Broken out by gender of respondent

Gender of respondent	No Answer	Not at all	Less than once a month	Monthly	Weekly	Several times a week	Daily
Male	13.75%	77.50%	5.00%	1.25%	2.50%	0.00%	0.00%
Female	10.00%	80.00%	6.00%	2.00%	0.00%	2.00%	0.00%
Other	0.00%	100.00%	0.00%	0.00%	0.00%	0.00%	0.00%

Table 1.1.6 How often do you use each of the following AI tools from major legal publishers? Lexis Brief Analyzer. Broken out by public or private law school

Public or private law school	No Answer	Not at all	Less than once a month	Monthly	Weekly	Several times a week	Daily
Public	13.58%	75.31%	6.17%	1.23%	2.47%	1.23%	0.00%
Private	9.43%	84.91%	3.77%	1.89%	0.00%	0.00%	0.00%

Table 1.1.7 How often do you use each of the following AI tools from major legal publishers? Lexis Brief Analyzer. Broken out by # of courses taught last semester

# of courses taught last semester	No Answer	Not at all	Less than once a month	Monthly	Weekly	Several times a week	Daily
None	14.81%	74.07%	3.70%	3.70%	0.00%	3.70%	0.00%
One	5.00%	80.00%	10.00%	2.50%	2.50%	0.00%	0.00%
Two	11.86%	83.05%	3.39%	0.00%	1.69%	0.00%	0.00%
More than two	37.50%	62.50%	0.00%	0.00%	0.00%	0.00%	0.00%

Table 1.1.8 How often do you use each of the following AI tools from major legal publishers? Lexis Brief Analyzer. Broken out by ranking

Ranking	No Answer	Not at all	Less than once a month	Monthly	Weekly	Several times a week	Daily
Top 20 law school	18.52%	70.37%	7.41%	0.00%	3.70%	0.00%	0.00%
Somewhere in the 21-75 rank	7.27%	80.00%	7.27%	3.64%	1.82%	0.00%	0.00%
76 to 250	8.70%	86.96%	2.17%	0.00%	0.00%	2.17%	0.00%
Other	50.00%	50.00%	0.00%	0.00%	0.00%	0.00%	0.00%

Table 1.1.9 How often do you use each of the following AI tools from major legal publishers? Lexis Brief Analyzer. Broken out by political views

Political views	No Answer	Not at all	Less than once a month	Monthly	Weekly	Several times a week	Daily
Conservative	14.29%	78.57%	0.00%	0.00%	7.14%	0.00%	0.00%
Centrist	20.59%	67.65%	5.88%	0.00%	2.94%	2.94%	0.00%
Liberal	6.15%	86.15%	4.62%	3.08%	0.00%	0.00%	0.00%
Left of Liberal	10.00%	80.00%	10.00%	0.00%	0.00%	0.00%	0.00%
Unknown	100.00%	0.00%	0.00%	0.00%	0.00%	0.00%	0.00%

Table 1.2.1 How often do you use each of the following AI tools from major legal publishers? Westlaw Edge.

	No Answer	Not at all	Less than once a month	Monthly	Weekly	Several times a week	Daily
Entire sample	10.45%	48.51%	14.93%	9.70%	8.96%	5.22%	2.24%

Table 1.2.2 How often do you use each of the following AI tools from major legal publishers? Westlaw Edge. Broken out by law school enrollment

Law school enrollment	No Answer	Not at all	Less than once a month	Monthly	Weekly	Several times a week	Daily
Less than 400	12.50%	56.25%	0.00%	18.75%	6.25%	3.13%	3.13%
400+ - 550	12.50%	37.50%	21.88%	6.25%	9.38%	12.50%	0.00%
550+ - 800	5.88%	52.94%	20.59%	2.94%	14.71%	0.00%	2.94%
More than 800	11.11%	47.22%	16.67%	11.11%	5.56%	5.56%	2.78%

Table 1.2.3 How often do you use each of the following AI tools from major legal publishers? Westlaw Edge. Broken out by academic title

Academic title	No Answer	Not at all	Less than once a month	Monthly	Weekly	Several times a week	Daily
Professor	9.84%	45.90%	11.48%	9.84%	16.39%	3.28%	3.28%
Assistant/ Associate Professor	9.52%	33.33%	19.05%	19.05%	4.76%	14.29%	0.00%
Adjunct/ Clinical Faculty	7.14%	60.71%	21.43%	7.14%	3.57%	0.00%	0.00%
Emeritus	13.33%	60.00%	13.33%	6.67%	0.00%	6.67%	0.00%
Other	22.22%	44.44%	11.11%	0.00%	0.00%	11.11%	11.11%

Table 1.2.4 How often do you use each of the following AI tools from major legal publishers? Westlaw Edge. Broken out by age of respondent

Age of respondent	No Answer	Not at all	Less than once a month	Monthly	Weekly	Several times a week	Daily
Under 40	16.67%	50.00%	16.67%	0.00%	0.00%	16.67%	0.00%
40-49	15.79%	42.11%	15.79%	21.05%	0.00%	5.26%	0.00%
50-59	0.00%	36.36%	21.21%	12.12%	18.18%	6.06%	6.06%
60 or over	13.33%	56.00%	12.00%	5.33%	8.00%	4.00%	1.33%
Unknown	0.00%	0.00%	0.00%	100.00%	0.00%	0.00%	0.00%

Table 1.2.5 How often do you use each of the following AI tools from major legal publishers? Westlaw Edge. Broken out by gender of respondent

Gender of respondent	No Answer	Not at all	Less than once a month	Monthly	Weekly	Several times a week	Daily
Male	12.50%	53.75%	15.00%	7.50%	7.50%	3.75%	0.00%
Female	8.00%	42.00%	14.00%	10.00%	12.00%	8.00%	6.00%
Other	0.00%	25.00%	25.00%	50.00%	0.00%	0.00%	0.00%

Table 1.2.6 How often do you use each of the following AI tools from major legal publishers? Westlaw Edge. Broken out by public or private law school

Public or private law school	No Answer	Not at all	Less than once a month	Monthly	Weekly	Several times a week	Daily
Public	13.58%	44.44%	16.05%	7.41%	8.64%	7.41%	2.47%
Private	5.66%	54.72%	13.21%	13.21%	9.43%	1.89%	1.89%

Table 1.2.7 How often do you use each of the following AI tools from major legal publishers? Westlaw Edge. Broken out by # of courses taught last semester

# of courses taught last semester	No Answer	Not at all	Less than once a month	Monthly	Weekly	Several times a week	Daily
None	11.11%	51.85%	22.22%	7.41%	0.00%	7.41%	0.00%
One	2.50%	57.50%	22.50%	5.00%	10.00%	0.00%	2.50%
Two	11.86%	42.37%	6.78%	13.56%	13.56%	8.47%	3.39%
More than two	37.50%	37.50%	12.50%	12.50%	0.00%	0.00%	0.00%

Table 1.2.8 How often do you use each of the following AI tools from major legal publishers? Westlaw Edge. Broken out by ranking

Ranking	No Answer	Not at all	Less than once a month	Monthly	Weekly	Several times a week	Daily
Top 20 law school	14.81%	59.26%	22.22%	0.00%	3.70%	0.00%	0.00%
Somewhere in the 21-75 rank	7.27%	50.91%	14.55%	9.09%	10.91%	3.64%	3.64%
76 to 250	8.70%	43.48%	13.04%	10.87%	10.87%	10.87%	2.17%
Other	33.33%	16.67%	0.00%	50.00%	0.00%	0.00%	0.00%

Table 1.2.9 How often do you use each of the following AI tools from major legal publishers? Westlaw Edge. Broken out by political views

Political views	No Answer	Not at all	Less than once a month	Monthly	Weekly	Several times a week	Daily
Conservative	7.14%	42.86%	21.43%	7.14%	21.43%	0.00%	0.00%
Centrist	17.65%	44.12%	8.82%	11.76%	5.88%	8.82%	2.94%
Liberal	6.15%	47.69%	15.38%	10.77%	10.77%	6.15%	3.08%
Left of Liberal	10.00%	65.00%	20.00%	5.00%	0.00%	0.00%	0.00%
Unknown	100.00%	0.00%	0.00%	0.00%	0.00%	0.00%	0.00%

Table 1.3.1 How often do you use each of the following AI tools from major legal publishers? CoCounsel.

	No Answer	Not at all	Less than once a month	Monthly	Weekly	Several times a week	Daily
Entire sample	13.43%	79.85%	3.73%	2.24%	0.00%	0.75%	0.00%

Table 1.3.2 How often do you use each of the following AI tools from major legal publishers? CoCounsel. Broken out by law school enrollment

Law school enrollment	No Answer	Not at all	Less than once a month	Monthly	Weekly	Several times a week	Daily
Less than 400	15.63%	81.25%	3.13%	0.00%	0.00%	0.00%	0.00%
400+ - 550	12.50%	78.13%	6.25%	3.13%	0.00%	0.00%	0.00%
550+ - 800	11.76%	82.35%	2.94%	2.94%	0.00%	0.00%	0.00%
More than 800	13.89%	77.78%	2.78%	2.78%	0.00%	2.78%	0.00%

Table 1.3.3 How often do you use each of the following AI tools from major legal publishers? CoCounsel. Broken out by academic title

Academic title	No Answer	Not at all	Less than once a month	Monthly	Weekly	Several times a week	Daily
Professor	11.48%	83.61%	3.28%	1.64%	0.00%	0.00%	0.00%
Assistant/ Associate Professor	9.52%	76.19%	4.76%	4.76%	0.00%	4.76%	0.00%
Adjunct/ Clinical Faculty	10.71%	82.14%	3.57%	3.57%	0.00%	0.00%	0.00%
Emeritus	26.67%	73.33%	0.00%	0.00%	0.00%	0.00%	0.00%
Other	22.22%	66.67%	11.11%	0.00%	0.00%	0.00%	0.00%

Table 1.3.4 How often do you use each of the following AI tools from major legal publishers? CoCounsel. Broken out by age of respondent

Age of respondent	No Answer	Not at all	Less than once a month	Monthly	Weekly	Several times a week	Daily
Under 40	16.67%	66.67%	0.00%	16.67%	0.00%	0.00%	0.00%
40-49	21.05%	68.42%	5.26%	5.26%	0.00%	0.00%	0.00%
50-59	3.03%	87.88%	3.03%	3.03%	0.00%	3.03%	0.00%
60 or over	16.00%	80.00%	4.00%	0.00%	0.00%	0.00%	0.00%
Unknown	0.00%	100.00%	0.00%	0.00%	0.00%	0.00%	0.00%

Table 1.3.5 How often do you use each of the following AI tools from major legal publishers? CoCounsel. Broken out by gender of respondent

Gender of respondent	No Answer	Not at all	Less than once a month	Monthly	Weekly	Several times a week	Daily
Male	16.25%	77.50%	5.00%	1.25%	0.00%	0.00%	0.00%
Female	10.00%	82.00%	2.00%	4.00%	0.00%	2.00%	0.00%
Other	0.00%	100.00%	0.00%	0.00%	0.00%	0.00%	0.00%

Table 1.3.6 How often do you use each of the following AI tools from major legal publishers? CoCounsel. Broken out by public or private law school

Public or private law school	No Answer	Not at all	Less than once a month	Monthly	Weekly	Several times a week	Daily
Public	16.05%	75.31%	4.94%	2.47%	0.00%	1.23%	0.00%
Private	9.43%	86.79%	1.89%	1.89%	0.00%	0.00%	0.00%

Table 1.3.7 How often do you use each of the following AI tools from major legal publishers? CoCounsel. Broken out by # of courses taught last semester

# of courses taught last semester	No Answer	Not at all	Less than once a month	Monthly	Weekly	Several times a week	Daily
None	22.22%	74.07%	0.00%	0.00%	0.00%	3.70%	0.00%
One	5.00%	82.50%	7.50%	5.00%	0.00%	0.00%	0.00%
Two	11.86%	84.75%	1.69%	1.69%	0.00%	0.00%	0.00%
More than two	37.50%	50.00%	12.50%	0.00%	0.00%	0.00%	0.00%

Table 1.3.8 How often do you use each of the following AI tools from major legal publishers? CoCounsel. Broken out by ranking

Ranking	No Answer	Not at all	Less than once a month	Monthly	Weekly	Several times a week	Daily
Top 20 law school	18.52%	74.07%	3.70%	3.70%	0.00%	0.00%	0.00%
Somewhere in the 21-75 rank	12.73%	81.82%	3.64%	1.82%	0.00%	0.00%	0.00%
76 to 250	8.70%	84.78%	4.35%	0.00%	0.00%	2.17%	0.00%
Other	33.33%	50.00%	0.00%	16.67%	0.00%	0.00%	0.00%

Table 1.3.9 How often do you use each of the following AI tools from major legal publishers? CoCounsel. Broken out by political views

Political views	No Answer	Not at all	Less than once a month	Monthly	Weekly	Several times a week	Daily
Conservative	14.29%	71.43%	7.14%	7.14%	0.00%	0.00%	0.00%
Centrist	23.53%	67.65%	5.88%	0.00%	0.00%	2.94%	0.00%
Liberal	7.69%	89.23%	0.00%	3.08%	0.00%	0.00%	0.00%
Left of Liberal	10.00%	80.00%	10.00%	0.00%	0.00%	0.00%	0.00%
Unknown	100.00%	0.00%	0.00%	0.00%	0.00%	0.00%	0.00%

Table 1.4.1 How often do you use each of the following AI tools from major legal publishers? Lexis+.

	No Answer	Not at all	Less than once a month	Monthly	Weekly	Several times a week	Daily
Entire sample	13.43%	61.19%	11.94%	8.21%	2.24%	2.24%	0.75%

Table 1.4.2 How often do you use each of the following AI tools from major legal publishers? Lexis+. Broken out by law school enrollment

Law school enrollment	No Answer	Not at all	Less than once a month	Monthly	Weekly	Several times a week	Daily
Less than 400	12.50%	62.50%	3.13%	12.50%	6.25%	0.00%	3.13%
400+ - 550	15.63%	56.25%	18.75%	6.25%	0.00%	3.13%	0.00%
550+ - 800	8.82%	70.59%	14.71%	5.88%	0.00%	0.00%	0.00%
More than 800	16.67%	55.56%	11.11%	8.33%	2.78%	5.56%	0.00%

Table 1.4.3 How often do you use each of the following AI tools from major legal publishers? Lexis+. Broken out by academic title

Academic title	No Answer	Not at all	Less than once a month	Monthly	Weekly	Several times a week	Daily
Professor	14.75%	63.93%	6.56%	8.20%	4.92%	1.64%	0.00%
Assistant/ Associate Professor	4.76%	52.38%	23.81%	14.29%	0.00%	4.76%	0.00%
Adjunct/ Clinical Faculty	10.71%	71.43%	10.71%	3.57%	0.00%	3.57%	0.00%
Emeritus	20.00%	53.33%	20.00%	6.67%	0.00%	0.00%	0.00%
Other	22.22%	44.44%	11.11%	11.11%	0.00%	0.00%	11.11%

Table 1.4.4 How often do you use each of the following AI tools from major legal publishers? Lexis+. Broken out by age of respondent

Age of respondent	No Answer	Not at all	Less than once a month	Monthly	Weekly	Several times a week	Daily
Under 40	0.00%	50.00%	16.67%	33.33%	0.00%	0.00%	0.00%
40-49	15.79%	57.89%	10.53%	10.53%	5.26%	0.00%	0.00%
50-59	6.06%	57.58%	18.18%	6.06%	6.06%	3.03%	3.03%
60 or over	17.33%	64.00%	9.33%	6.67%	0.00%	2.67%	0.00%
Unknown	0.00%	100.00%	0.00%	0.00%	0.00%	0.00%	0.00%

Table 1.4.5 How often do you use each of the following AI tools from major legal publishers? Lexis+. Broken out by gender of respondent

Gender of respondent	No Answer	Not at all	Less than once a month	Monthly	Weekly	Several times a week	Daily
Male	16.25%	62.50%	10.00%	7.50%	1.25%	2.50%	0.00%
Female	10.00%	58.00%	16.00%	8.00%	4.00%	2.00%	2.00%
Other	0.00%	75.00%	0.00%	25.00%	0.00%	0.00%	0.00%

Table 1.4.6 How often do you use each of the following AI tools from major legal publishers? Lexis+. Broken out by public or private law school

Public or private law school	No Answer	Not at all	Less than once a month	Monthly	Weekly	Several times a week	Daily
Public	14.81%	58.02%	14.81%	6.17%	2.47%	2.47%	1.23%
Private	11.32%	66.04%	7.55%	11.32%	1.89%	1.89%	0.00%

Table 1.4.7 How often do you use each of the following AI tools from major legal publishers? Lexis+. Broken out by # of courses taught last semester

# of courses taught last semester	No Answer	Not at all	Less than once a month	Monthly	Weekly	Several times a week	Daily
None	22.22%	55.56%	14.81%	3.70%	0.00%	3.70%	0.00%
One	2.50%	65.00%	20.00%	7.50%	2.50%	0.00%	2.50%
Two	13.56%	62.71%	6.78%	10.17%	3.39%	3.39%	0.00%
More than two	37.50%	50.00%	0.00%	12.50%	0.00%	0.00%	0.00%

Table 1.4.8 How often do you use each of the following AI tools from major legal publishers? Lexis+. Broken out by ranking

Ranking	No Answer	Not at all	Less than once a month	Monthly	Weekly	Several times a week	Daily
Top 20 law school	22.22%	55.56%	11.11%	11.11%	0.00%	0.00%	0.00%
Somewhere in the 21-75 rank	10.91%	58.18%	18.18%	5.45%	1.82%	3.64%	1.82%
76 to 250	6.52%	71.74%	6.52%	8.70%	4.35%	2.17%	0.00%
Other	50.00%	33.33%	0.00%	16.67%	0.00%	0.00%	0.00%

Table 1.4.9 How often do you use each of the following AI tools from major legal publishers? Lexis+. Broken out by political views

Political views	No Answer	Not at all	Less than once a month	Monthly	Weekly	Several times a week	Daily
Conservative	14.29%	64.29%	7.14%	7.14%	0.00%	7.14%	0.00%
Centrist	23.53%	58.82%	2.94%	5.88%	2.94%	2.94%	2.94%
Liberal	9.23%	60.00%	16.92%	9.23%	3.08%	1.54%	0.00%
Left of Liberal	5.00%	70.00%	15.00%	10.00%	0.00%	0.00%	0.00%
Unknown	100.00%	0.00%	0.00%	0.00%	0.00%	0.00%	0.00%

Table 1.5.1 How often do you use each of the following AI tools from major legal publishers? Bloomberg Draft Analyzer.

	No Answer	Not at all	Less than once a month	Monthly	Weekly	Several times a week	Daily
Entire sample	15.67%	83.58%	0.75%	0.00%	0.00%	0.00%	0.00%

Table 1.5.2 How often do you use each of the following AI tools from major legal publishers? Bloomberg Draft Analyzer. Broken out by law school enrollment

Law school enrollment	No Answer	Not at all	Less than once a month	Monthly	Weekly	Several times a week	Daily
Less than 400	15.63%	81.25%	3.13%	0.00%	0.00%	0.00%	0.00%
400+ - 550	15.63%	84.38%	0.00%	0.00%	0.00%	0.00%	0.00%
550+ - 800	11.76%	88.24%	0.00%	0.00%	0.00%	0.00%	0.00%
More than 800	19.44%	80.56%	0.00%	0.00%	0.00%	0.00%	0.00%

Table 1.5.3 How often do you use each of the following AI tools from major legal publishers? Bloomberg Draft Analyzer. Broken out by academic title

Academic title	No Answer	Not at all	Less than once a month	Monthly	Weekly	Several times a week	Daily
Professor	13.11%	86.89%	0.00%	0.00%	0.00%	0.00%	0.00%
Assistant/ Associate Professor	14.29%	85.71%	0.00%	0.00%	0.00%	0.00%	0.00%
Adjunct/ Clinical Faculty	10.71%	89.29%	0.00%	0.00%	0.00%	0.00%	0.00%
Emeritus	33.33%	66.67%	0.00%	0.00%	0.00%	0.00%	0.00%
Other	22.22%	66.67%	11.11%	0.00%	0.00%	0.00%	0.00%

Table 1.5.4 How often do you use each of the following AI tools from major legal publishers? Bloomberg Draft Analyzer. Broken out by age of respondent

Age of respondent	No Answer	Not at all	Less than once a month	Monthly	Weekly	Several times a week	Daily
Under 40	16.67%	83.33%	0.00%	0.00%	0.00%	0.00%	0.00%
40-49	21.05%	78.95%	0.00%	0.00%	0.00%	0.00%	0.00%
50-59	6.06%	90.91%	3.03%	0.00%	0.00%	0.00%	0.00%
60 or over	18.67%	81.33%	0.00%	0.00%	0.00%	0.00%	0.00%
Unknown	0.00%	100.00%	0.00%	0.00%	0.00%	0.00%	0.00%

Table 1.5.5 How often do you use each of the following AI tools from major legal publishers? Bloomberg Draft Analyzer. Broken out by gender of respondent

Gender of respondent	No Answer	Not at all	Less than once a month	Monthly	Weekly	Several times a week	Daily
Male	20.00%	80.00%	0.00%	0.00%	0.00%	0.00%	0.00%
Female	10.00%	88.00%	2.00%	0.00%	0.00%	0.00%	0.00%
Other	0.00%	100.00%	0.00%	0.00%	0.00%	0.00%	0.00%

Table 1.5.6 How often do you use each of the following AI tools from major legal publishers? Bloomberg Draft Analyzer. Broken out by public or private law school

Public or private law school	No Answer	Not at all	Less than once a month	Monthly	Weekly	Several times a week	Daily
Public	17.28%	81.48%	1.23%	0.00%	0.00%	0.00%	0.00%
Private	13.21%	86.79%	0.00%	0.00%	0.00%	0.00%	0.00%

Table 1.5.7 How often do you use each of the following AI tools from major legal publishers? Bloomberg Draft Analyzer. Broken out by # of courses taught last semester

# of courses taught last semester	No Answer	Not at all	Less than once a month	Monthly	Weekly	Several times a week	Daily
None	29.63%	70.37%	0.00%	0.00%	0.00%	0.00%	0.00%
One	5.00%	92.50%	2.50%	0.00%	0.00%	0.00%	0.00%
Two	13.56%	86.44%	0.00%	0.00%	0.00%	0.00%	0.00%
More than two	37.50%	62.50%	0.00%	0.00%	0.00%	0.00%	0.00%

Table 1.5.8 How often do you use each of the following AI tools from major legal publishers? Bloomberg Draft Analyzer. Broken out by ranking

Ranking	No Answer	Not at all	Less than once a month	Monthly	Weekly	Several times a week	Daily
Top 20 law school	22.22%	77.78%	0.00%	0.00%	0.00%	0.00%	0.00%
Somewhere in the 21-75 rank	14.55%	83.64%	1.82%	0.00%	0.00%	0.00%	0.00%
76 to 250	8.70%	91.30%	0.00%	0.00%	0.00%	0.00%	0.00%
Other	50.00%	50.00%	0.00%	0.00%	0.00%	0.00%	0.00%

Table 1.5.9 How often do you use each of the following AI tools from major legal publishers? Bloomberg Draft Analyzer. Broken out by political views

Political views	No Answer	Not at all	Less than once a month	Monthly	Weekly	Several times a week	Daily
Conservative	21.43%	78.57%	0.00%	0.00%	0.00%	0.00%	0.00%
Centrist	23.53%	73.53%	2.94%	0.00%	0.00%	0.00%	0.00%
Liberal	10.77%	89.23%	0.00%	0.00%	0.00%	0.00%	0.00%
Left of Liberal	10.00%	90.00%	0.00%	0.00%	0.00%	0.00%	0.00%
Unknown	100.00%	0.00%	0.00%	0.00%	0.00%	0.00%	0.00%

Table 1.6.1 How often do you use each of the following AI tools from major legal publishers? Fastcase.

	No Answer	Not at all	Less than once a month	Monthly	Weekly	Several times a week	Daily
Entire sample	14.93%	76.12%	5.22%	1.49%	1.49%	0.75%	0.00%

Table 1.6.2 How often do you use each of the following AI tools from major legal publishers? Fastcase. Broken out by law school enrollment

Law school enrollment	No Answer	Not at all	Less than once a month	Monthly	Weekly	Several times a week	Daily
Less than 400	15.63%	65.63%	12.50%	0.00%	3.13%	3.13%	0.00%
400+ - 550	12.50%	87.50%	0.00%	0.00%	0.00%	0.00%	0.00%
550+ - 800	11.76%	76.47%	5.88%	2.94%	2.94%	0.00%	0.00%
More than 800	19.44%	75.00%	2.78%	2.78%	0.00%	0.00%	0.00%

Table 1.6.3 How often do you use each of the following AI tools from major legal publishers? Fastcase. Broken out by academic title

Academic title	No Answer	Not at all	Less than once a month	Monthly	Weekly	Several times a week	Daily
Professor	13.11%	83.61%	1.64%	1.64%	0.00%	0.00%	0.00%
Assistant/ Associate Professor	9.52%	76.19%	14.29%	0.00%	0.00%	0.00%	0.00%
Adjunct/ Clinical Faculty	10.71%	67.86%	7.14%	3.57%	7.14%	3.57%	0.00%
Emeritus	33.33%	66.67%	0.00%	0.00%	0.00%	0.00%	0.00%
Other	22.22%	66.67%	11.11%	0.00%	0.00%	0.00%	0.00%

Table 1.6.4 How often do you use each of the following AI tools from major legal publishers? Fastcase. Broken out by age of respondent

Age of respondent	No Answer	Not at all	Less than once a month	Monthly	Weekly	Several times a week	Daily
Under 40	16.67%	66.67%	16.67%	0.00%	0.00%	0.00%	0.00%
40-49	15.79%	78.95%	0.00%	0.00%	0.00%	5.26%	0.00%
50-59	6.06%	81.82%	6.06%	0.00%	6.06%	0.00%	0.00%
60 or over	18.67%	74.67%	4.00%	2.67%	0.00%	0.00%	0.00%
Unknown	0.00%	0.00%	100.00%	0.00%	0.00%	0.00%	0.00%

Table 1.6.5 How often do you use each of the following AI tools from major legal publishers? Fastcase. Broken out by gender of respondent

Gender of respondent	No Answer	Not at all	Less than once a month	Monthly	Weekly	Several times a week	Daily
Male	18.75%	77.50%	2.50%	0.00%	1.25%	0.00%	0.00%
Female	10.00%	76.00%	8.00%	2.00%	2.00%	2.00%	0.00%
Other	0.00%	50.00%	25.00%	25.00%	0.00%	0.00%	0.00%

Table 1.6.6 How often do you use each of the following AI tools from major legal publishers? Fastcase. Broken out by public or private law school

Public or private law school	No Answer	Not at all	Less than once a month	Monthly	Weekly	Several times a week	Daily
Public	16.05%	71.60%	8.64%	0.00%	2.47%	1.23%	0.00%
Private	13.21%	83.02%	0.00%	3.77%	0.00%	0.00%	0.00%

Table 1.6.7 How often do you use each of the following AI tools from major legal publishers? Fastcase. Broken out by # of courses taught last semester

# of courses taught last semester	No Answer	Not at all	Less than once a month	Monthly	Weekly	Several times a week	Daily
None	29.63%	62.96%	3.70%	3.70%	0.00%	0.00%	0.00%
One	5.00%	82.50%	2.50%	2.50%	5.00%	2.50%	0.00%
Two	11.86%	79.66%	8.47%	0.00%	0.00%	0.00%	0.00%
More than two	37.50%	62.50%	0.00%	0.00%	0.00%	0.00%	0.00%

Table 1.6.8 How often do you use each of the following AI tools from major legal publishers? Fastcase. Broken out by ranking

Ranking	No Answer	Not at all	Less than once a month	Monthly	Weekly	Several times a week	Daily
Top 20 law school	22.22%	70.37%	3.70%	3.70%	0.00%	0.00%	0.00%
Somewhere in the 21-75 rank	12.73%	83.64%	0.00%	1.82%	0.00%	1.82%	0.00%
76 to 250	8.70%	73.91%	13.04%	0.00%	4.35%	0.00%	0.00%
Other	50.00%	50.00%	0.00%	0.00%	0.00%	0.00%	0.00%

Table 1.6.9 How often do you use each of the following AI tools from major legal publishers? Fastcase. Broken out by political views

Political views	No Answer	Not at all	Less than once a month	Monthly	Weekly	Several times a week	Daily
Conservative	14.29%	85.71%	0.00%	0.00%	0.00%	0.00%	0.00%
Centrist	23.53%	67.65%	8.82%	0.00%	0.00%	0.00%	0.00%
Liberal	10.77%	76.92%	4.62%	3.08%	3.08%	1.54%	0.00%
Left of Liberal	10.00%	85.00%	5.00%	0.00%	0.00%	0.00%	0.00%
Unknown	100.00%	0.00%	0.00%	0.00%	0.00%	0.00%	0.00%

Table 1.7.1 How often do you use each of the following AI tools from major legal publishers? LawGeex.

	No Answer	Not at all	Less than once a month	Monthly	Weekly	Several times a week	Daily
Entire sample	14.93%	83.58%	1.49%	0.00%	0.00%	0.00%	0.00%

Table 1.7.2 How often do you use each of the following AI tools from major legal publishers? LawGeex. Broken out by law school enrollment

Law school enrollment	No Answer	Not at all	Less than once a month	Monthly	Weekly	Several times a week	Daily
Less than 400	15.63%	84.38%	0.00%	0.00%	0.00%	0.00%	0.00%
400+ - 550	12.50%	87.50%	0.00%	0.00%	0.00%	0.00%	0.00%
550+ - 800	11.76%	85.29%	2.94%	0.00%	0.00%	0.00%	0.00%
More than 800	19.44%	77.78%	2.78%	0.00%	0.00%	0.00%	0.00%

Table 1.7.3 How often do you use each of the following AI tools from major legal publishers? LawGeex. Broken out by academic title

Academic title	No Answer	Not at all	Less than once a month	Monthly	Weekly	Several times a week	Daily
Professor	13.11%	85.25%	1.64%	0.00%	0.00%	0.00%	0.00%
Assistant/ Associate Professor	9.52%	90.48%	0.00%	0.00%	0.00%	0.00%	0.00%
Adjunct/ Clinical Faculty	10.71%	85.71%	3.57%	0.00%	0.00%	0.00%	0.00%
Emeritus	33.33%	66.67%	0.00%	0.00%	0.00%	0.00%	0.00%
Other	22.22%	77.78%	0.00%	0.00%	0.00%	0.00%	0.00%

Table 1.7.4 How often do you use each of the following AI tools from major legal publishers? LawGeex. Broken out by age of respondent

Age of respondent	No Answer	Not at all	Less than once a month	Monthly	Weekly	Several times a week	Daily
Under 40	16.67%	83.33%	0.00%	0.00%	0.00%	0.00%	0.00%
40-49	15.79%	84.21%	0.00%	0.00%	0.00%	0.00%	0.00%
50-59	6.06%	90.91%	3.03%	0.00%	0.00%	0.00%	0.00%
60 or over	18.67%	80.00%	1.33%	0.00%	0.00%	0.00%	0.00%
Unknown	0.00%	100.00%	0.00%	0.00%	0.00%	0.00%	0.00%

Table 1.7.5 How often do you use each of the following AI tools from major legal publishers? LawGeex. Broken out by gender of respondent

Gender of respondent	No Answer	Not at all	Less than once a month	Monthly	Weekly	Several times a week	Daily
Male	18.75%	81.25%	0.00%	0.00%	0.00%	0.00%	0.00%
Female	10.00%	88.00%	2.00%	0.00%	0.00%	0.00%	0.00%
Other	0.00%	75.00%	25.00%	0.00%	0.00%	0.00%	0.00%

Table 1.7.6 How often do you use each of the following AI tools from major legal publishers? LawGeex. Broken out by public or private law school

Public or private law school	No Answer	Not at all	Less than once a month	Monthly	Weekly	Several times a week	Daily
Public	16.05%	83.95%	0.00%	0.00%	0.00%	0.00%	0.00%
Private	13.21%	83.02%	3.77%	0.00%	0.00%	0.00%	0.00%

Table 1.7.7 How often do you use each of the following AI tools from major legal publishers? LawGeex. Broken out by # of courses taught last semester

# of courses taught last semester	No Answer	Not at all	Less than once a month	Monthly	Weekly	Several times a week	Daily
None	29.63%	66.67%	3.70%	0.00%	0.00%	0.00%	0.00%
One	5.00%	95.00%	0.00%	0.00%	0.00%	0.00%	0.00%
Two	11.86%	86.44%	1.69%	0.00%	0.00%	0.00%	0.00%
More than two	37.50%	62.50%	0.00%	0.00%	0.00%	0.00%	0.00%

Table 1.7.8 How often do you use each of the following AI tools from major legal publishers? LawGeex. Broken out by ranking

Ranking	No Answer	Not at all	Less than once a month	Monthly	Weekly	Several times a week	Daily
Top 20 law school	22.22%	74.07%	3.70%	0.00%	0.00%	0.00%	0.00%
Somewhere in the 21-75 rank	12.73%	85.45%	1.82%	0.00%	0.00%	0.00%	0.00%
76 to 250	8.70%	91.30%	0.00%	0.00%	0.00%	0.00%	0.00%
Other	50.00%	50.00%	0.00%	0.00%	0.00%	0.00%	0.00%

Table 1.7.9 How often do you use each of the following AI tools from major legal publishers? LawGeex. Broken out by political views

Political views	No Answer	Not at all	Less than once a month	Monthly	Weekly	Several times a week	Daily
Conservative	14.29%	85.71%	0.00%	0.00%	0.00%	0.00%	0.00%
Centrist	23.53%	76.47%	0.00%	0.00%	0.00%	0.00%	0.00%
Liberal	10.77%	86.15%	3.08%	0.00%	0.00%	0.00%	0.00%
Left of Liberal	10.00%	90.00%	0.00%	0.00%	0.00%	0.00%	0.00%
Unknown	100.00%	0.00%	0.00%	0.00%	0.00%	0.00%	0.00%

Table 1.8.1 How often do you use each of the following AI tools from major legal publishers? EverLaw.

	No Answer	Not at all	Less than once a month	Monthly	Weekly	Several times a week	Daily
Entire sample	14.93%	83.58%	0.75%	0.75%	0.00%	0.00%	0.00%

Table 1.8.2 How often do you use each of the following AI tools from major legal publishers? EverLaw. Broken out by law school enrollment

Law school enrollment	No Answer	Not at all	Less than once a month	Monthly	Weekly	Several times a week	Daily
Less than 400	15.63%	81.25%	3.13%	0.00%	0.00%	0.00%	0.00%
400+ - 550	12.50%	87.50%	0.00%	0.00%	0.00%	0.00%	0.00%
550+ - 800	11.76%	85.29%	0.00%	2.94%	0.00%	0.00%	0.00%
More than 800	19.44%	80.56%	0.00%	0.00%	0.00%	0.00%	0.00%

Table 1.8.3 How often do you use each of the following AI tools from major legal publishers? EverLaw. Broken out by academic title

Academic title	No Answer	Not at all	Less than once a month	Monthly	Weekly	Several times a week	Daily
Professor	13.11%	85.25%	0.00%	1.64%	0.00%	0.00%	0.00%
Assistant/ Associate Professor	9.52%	90.48%	0.00%	0.00%	0.00%	0.00%	0.00%
Adjunct/ Clinical Faculty	10.71%	85.71%	3.57%	0.00%	0.00%	0.00%	0.00%
Emeritus	33.33%	66.67%	0.00%	0.00%	0.00%	0.00%	0.00%
Other	22.22%	77.78%	0.00%	0.00%	0.00%	0.00%	0.00%

Table 1.8.4 How often do you use each of the following AI tools from major legal publishers? EverLaw. Broken out by age of respondent

Age of respondent	No Answer	Not at all	Less than once a month	Monthly	Weekly	Several times a week	Daily
Under 40	16.67%	83.33%	0.00%	0.00%	0.00%	0.00%	0.00%
40-49	15.79%	84.21%	0.00%	0.00%	0.00%	0.00%	0.00%
50-59	6.06%	90.91%	3.03%	0.00%	0.00%	0.00%	0.00%
60 or over	18.67%	80.00%	0.00%	1.33%	0.00%	0.00%	0.00%
Unknown	0.00%	100.00%	0.00%	0.00%	0.00%	0.00%	0.00%

Table 1.8.5 How often do you use each of the following AI tools from major legal publishers? EverLaw. Broken out by gender of respondent

Gender of respondent	No Answer	Not at all	Less than once a month	Monthly	Weekly	Several times a week	Daily
Male	18.75%	81.25%	0.00%	0.00%	0.00%	0.00%	0.00%
Female	10.00%	86.00%	2.00%	2.00%	0.00%	0.00%	0.00%
Other	0.00%	100.00%	0.00%	0.00%	0.00%	0.00%	0.00%

Table 1.8.6 How often do you use each of the following AI tools from major legal publishers? EverLaw. Broken out by public or private law school

Public or private law school	No Answer	Not at all	Less than once a month	Monthly	Weekly	Several times a week	Daily
Public	16.05%	82.72%	1.23%	0.00%	0.00%	0.00%	0.00%
Private	13.21%	84.91%	0.00%	1.89%	0.00%	0.00%	0.00%

Table 1.8.7 How often do you use each of the following AI tools from major legal publishers? EverLaw. Broken out by # of courses taught last semester

# of courses taught last semester	No Answer	Not at all	Less than once a month	Monthly	Weekly	Several times a week	Daily
None	29.63%	66.67%	3.70%	0.00%	0.00%	0.00%	0.00%
One	5.00%	92.50%	0.00%	2.50%	0.00%	0.00%	0.00%
Two	11.86%	88.14%	0.00%	0.00%	0.00%	0.00%	0.00%
More than two	37.50%	62.50%	0.00%	0.00%	0.00%	0.00%	0.00%

Table 1.8.8 How often do you use each of the following AI tools from major legal publishers? EverLaw. Broken out by ranking

Ranking	No Answer	Not at all	Less than once a month	Monthly	Weekly	Several times a week	Daily
Top 20 law school	22.22%	77.78%	0.00%	0.00%	0.00%	0.00%	0.00%
Somewhere in the 21-75 rank	12.73%	85.45%	0.00%	1.82%	0.00%	0.00%	0.00%
76 to 250	8.70%	89.13%	2.17%	0.00%	0.00%	0.00%	0.00%
Other	50.00%	50.00%	0.00%	0.00%	0.00%	0.00%	0.00%

Table 1.8.9 How often do you use each of the following AI tools from major legal publishers? EverLaw. Broken out by political views

Political views	No Answer	Not at all	Less than once a month	Monthly	Weekly	Several times a week	Daily
Conservative	14.29%	85.71%	0.00%	0.00%	0.00%	0.00%	0.00%
Centrist	23.53%	73.53%	2.94%	0.00%	0.00%	0.00%	0.00%
Liberal	10.77%	87.69%	0.00%	1.54%	0.00%	0.00%	0.00%
Left of Liberal	10.00%	90.00%	0.00%	0.00%	0.00%	0.00%	0.00%
Unknown	100.00%	0.00%	0.00%	0.00%	0.00%	0.00%	0.00%

Table 1.9.1 How often do you use each of the following AI tools from major legal publishers? Luminance.

	No Answer	Not at all	Less than once a month	Monthly	Weekly	Several times a week	Daily
Entire sample	14.93%	85.07%	0.00%	0.00%	0.00%	0.00%	0.00%

Table 1.9.2 How often do you use each of the following AI tools from major legal publishers? Luminance. Broken out by law school enrollment

Law school enrollment	No Answer	Not at all	Less than once a month	Monthly	Weekly	Several times a week	Daily
Less than 400	15.63%	84.38%	0.00%	0.00%	0.00%	0.00%	0.00%
400+ - 550	12.50%	87.50%	0.00%	0.00%	0.00%	0.00%	0.00%
550+ - 800	11.76%	88.24%	0.00%	0.00%	0.00%	0.00%	0.00%
More than 800	19.44%	80.56%	0.00%	0.00%	0.00%	0.00%	0.00%

Table 1.9.3 How often do you use each of the following AI tools from major legal publishers? Luminance. Broken out by academic title

Academic title	No Answer	Not at all	Less than once a month	Monthly	Weekly	Several times a week
Professor	13.11%	86.89%	0.00%	0.00%	0.00%	0.00%
Assistant/Associate Professor	9.52%	90.48%	0.00%	0.00%	0.00%	0.00%
Adjunct/Clinical Faculty	10.71%	89.29%	0.00%	0.00%	0.00%	0.00%
Emeritus	33.33%	66.67%	0.00%	0.00%	0.00%	0.00%
Other	22.22%	77.78%	0.00%	0.00%	0.00%	0.00%

Table 1.9.4 How often do you use each of the following AI tools from major legal publishers? Luminance. Broken out by age of respondent

Age of respondent	No Answer	Not at all	Less than once a month	Monthly	Weekly	Several times a week	Daily
Under 40	16.67%	83.33%	0.00%	0.00%	0.00%	0.00%	0.00%
40-49	15.79%	84.21%	0.00%	0.00%	0.00%	0.00%	0.00%
50-59	6.06%	93.94%	0.00%	0.00%	0.00%	0.00%	0.00%
60 or over	18.67%	81.33%	0.00%	0.00%	0.00%	0.00%	0.00%
Unknown	0.00%	100.00%	0.00%	0.00%	0.00%	0.00%	0.00%

Table 1.9.5 How often do you use each of the following AI tools from major legal publishers? Luminance. Broken out by gender of respondent

Gender of respondent	No Answer	Not at all	Less than once a month	Monthly	Weekly	Several times a week	Daily
Male	18.75%	81.25%	0.00%	0.00%	0.00%	0.00%	0.00%
Female	10.00%	90.00%	0.00%	0.00%	0.00%	0.00%	0.00%
Other	0.00%	100.00%	0.00%	0.00%	0.00%	0.00%	0.00%

Table 1.9.6 How often do you use each of the following AI tools from major legal publishers? Luminance. Broken out by public or private law school

Public or private law school	No Answer	Not at all	Less than once a month	Monthly	Weekly	Several times a week	Daily
Public	16.05%	83.95%	0.00%	0.00%	0.00%	0.00%	0.00%
Private	13.21%	86.79%	0.00%	0.00%	0.00%	0.00%	0.00%

Table 1.9.7 How often do you use each of the following AI tools from major legal publishers? Luminance. Broken out by # of courses taught last semester

# of courses taught last semester	No Answer	Not at all	Less than once a month	Monthly	Weekly	Several times a week	Daily
None	29.63%	70.37%	0.00%	0.00%	0.00%	0.00%	0.00%
One	5.00%	95.00%	0.00%	0.00%	0.00%	0.00%	0.00%
Two	11.86%	88.14%	0.00%	0.00%	0.00%	0.00%	0.00%
More than two	37.50%	62.50%	0.00%	0.00%	0.00%	0.00%	0.00%

Table 1.9.8 How often do you use each of the following AI tools from major legal publishers? Luminance. Broken out by ranking

Ranking	No Answer	Not at all	Less than once a month	Monthly	Weekly	Several times a week	Daily
Top 20 law school	22.22%	77.78%	0.00%	0.00%	0.00%	0.00%	0.00%
Somewhere in the 21-75 rank	12.73%	87.27%	0.00%	0.00%	0.00%	0.00%	0.00%
76 to 250	8.70%	91.30%	0.00%	0.00%	0.00%	0.00%	0.00%
Other	50.00%	50.00%	0.00%	0.00%	0.00%	0.00%	0.00%

Table 1.9.9 How often do you use each of the following AI tools from major legal publishers? Luminance. Broken out by political views

Political views	No Answer	Not at all	Less than once a month	Monthly	Weekly	Several times a week	Daily
Conservative	14.29%	85.71%	0.00%	0.00%	0.00%	0.00%	0.00%
Centrist	23.53%	76.47%	0.00%	0.00%	0.00%	0.00%	0.00%
Liberal	10.77%	89.23%	0.00%	0.00%	0.00%	0.00%	0.00%
Left of Liberal	10.00%	90.00%	0.00%	0.00%	0.00%	0.00%	0.00%
Unknown	100.00%	0.00%	0.00%	0.00%	0.00%	0.00%	0.00%

Table 1.10.1 How often do you use each of the following AI tools from major legal publishers? DoNotPay.

	No Answer	Not at all	Less than once a month	Monthly	Weekly	Several times a week	Daily
Entire sample	15.67%	82.84%	1.49%	0.00%	0.00%	0.00%	0.00%

Table 1.10.2 How often do you use each of the following AI tools from major legal publishers? DoNotPay. Broken out by law school enrollment

Law school enrollment	No Answer	Not at all	Less than once a month	Monthly	Weekly	Several times a week	Daily
Less than 400	15.63%	84.38%	0.00%	0.00%	0.00%	0.00%	0.00%
400+ - 550	12.50%	87.50%	0.00%	0.00%	0.00%	0.00%	0.00%
550+ - 800	14.71%	85.29%	0.00%	0.00%	0.00%	0.00%	0.00%
More than 800	19.44%	75.00%	5.56%	0.00%	0.00%	0.00%	0.00%

Table 1.10.3 How often do you use each of the following AI tools from major legal publishers? DoNotPay. Broken out by academic title

Academic title	No Answer	Not at all	Less than once a month	Monthly	Weekly	Several times a week	Daily
Professor	14.75%	85.25%	0.00%	0.00%	0.00%	0.00%	0.00%
Assistant/ Associate Professor	9.52%	90.48%	0.00%	0.00%	0.00%	0.00%	0.00%
Adjunct/ Clinical Faculty	10.71%	82.14%	7.14%	0.00%	0.00%	0.00%	0.00%
Emeritus	33.33%	66.67%	0.00%	0.00%	0.00%	0.00%	0.00%
Other	22.22%	77.78%	0.00%	0.00%	0.00%	0.00%	0.00%

Table 1.10.4 How often do you use each of the following AI tools from major legal publishers? DoNotPay. Broken out by age of respondent

Age of respondent	No Answer	Not at all	Less than once a month	Monthly	Weekly	Several times a week	Daily
Under 40	16.67%	83.33%	0.00%	0.00%	0.00%	0.00%	0.00%
40-49	15.79%	84.21%	0.00%	0.00%	0.00%	0.00%	0.00%
50-59	9.09%	90.91%	0.00%	0.00%	0.00%	0.00%	0.00%
60 or over	18.67%	78.67%	2.67%	0.00%	0.00%	0.00%	0.00%
Unknown	0.00%	100.00%	0.00%	0.00%	0.00%	0.00%	0.00%

Table 1.10.5 How often do you use each of the following AI tools from major legal publishers? DoNotPay. Broken out by gender of respondent

Gender of respondent	No Answer	Not at all	Less than once a month	Monthly	Weekly	Several times a week	Daily
Male	18.75%	80.00%	1.25%	0.00%	0.00%	0.00%	0.00%
Female	12.00%	88.00%	0.00%	0.00%	0.00%	0.00%	0.00%
Other	0.00%	75.00%	25.00%	0.00%	0.00%	0.00%	0.00%

Table 1.10.6 How often do you use each of the following AI tools from major legal publishers? DoNotPay. Broken out by public or private law school

Public or private law school	No Answer	Not at all	Less than once a month	Monthly	Weekly	Several times a week	Daily
Public	16.05%	82.72%	1.23%	0.00%	0.00%	0.00%	0.00%
Private	15.09%	83.02%	1.89%	0.00%	0.00%	0.00%	0.00%

Table 1.10.7 How often do you use each of the following AI tools from major legal publishers? DoNotPay. Broken out by # of courses taught last semester

# of courses taught last semester	No Answer	Not at all	Less than once a month	Monthly	Weekly	Several times a week	Daily
None	29.63%	66.67%	3.70%	0.00%	0.00%	0.00%	0.00%
One	5.00%	92.50%	2.50%	0.00%	0.00%	0.00%	0.00%
Two	13.56%	86.44%	0.00%	0.00%	0.00%	0.00%	0.00%
More than two	37.50%	62.50%	0.00%	0.00%	0.00%	0.00%	0.00%

Table 1.10.8 How often do you use each of the following AI tools from major legal publishers? DoNotPay. Broken out by ranking

Ranking	No Answer	Not at all	Less than once a month	Monthly	Weekly	Several times a week	Daily
Top 20 law school	22.22%	70.37%	7.41%	0.00%	0.00%	0.00%	0.00%
Somewhere in the 21-75 rank	14.55%	85.45%	0.00%	0.00%	0.00%	0.00%	0.00%
76 to 250	8.70%	91.30%	0.00%	0.00%	0.00%	0.00%	0.00%
Other	50.00%	50.00%	0.00%	0.00%	0.00%	0.00%	0.00%

Table 1.10.9 How often do you use each of the following AI tools from major legal publishers? DoNotPay. Broken out by political views

Political views	No Answer	Not at all	Less than once a month	Monthly	Weekly	Several times a week	Daily
Conservative	14.29%	78.57%	7.14%	0.00%	0.00%	0.00%	0.00%
Centrist	23.53%	76.47%	0.00%	0.00%	0.00%	0.00%	0.00%
Liberal	12.31%	86.15%	1.54%	0.00%	0.00%	0.00%	0.00%
Left of Liberal	10.00%	90.00%	0.00%	0.00%	0.00%	0.00%	0.00%
Unknown	100.00%	0.00%	0.00%	0.00%	0.00%	0.00%	0.00%

Table 2 If you use Westlaw Edge, rate the usefulness to you of the following features: Westlaw ANswers

Table 2.1.1 If you use Westlaw Edge, rate the usefulness to you of the following features. Westlaw Answers.

	No Answer	Essential	Highly Useful	Often Useful	Sometimes Useful	Not really Useful	Not really familiar with this feature
Entire sample	45.52%	0.00%	5.22%	5.22%	8.96%	4.48%	30.60%

Table 2.1.2 If you use Westlaw Edge, rate the usefulness to you of the following features. Westlaw Answers. Broken out by law school enrollment

Law school enrollment	No Answer	Essential	Highly Useful	Often Useful	Sometimes Useful	Not really Useful	Not really familiar with this feature
Less than 400	59.38%	0.00%	3.13%	6.25%	9.38%	0.00%	21.88%
400+ - 550	40.63%	0.00%	6.25%	3.13%	9.38%	6.25%	34.38%
550+ - 800	38.24%	0.00%	8.82%	5.88%	8.82%	11.76%	26.47%
More than 800	44.44%	0.00%	2.78%	5.56%	8.33%	0.00%	38.89%

Table 2.1.3 If you use Westlaw Edge, rate the usefulness to you of the following features. Westlaw Answers. Broken out by academic title

Academic title	No Answer	Essential	Highly Useful	Often Useful	Sometimes Useful	Not really Useful	Not really familiar with this feature
Professor	47.54%	0.00%	8.20%	3.28%	6.56%	3.28%	31.15%
Assistant/ Associate Professor	23.81%	0.00%	0.00%	9.52%	9.52%	9.52%	47.62%
Adjunct/ Clinical Faculty	50.00%	0.00%	3.57%	7.14%	14.29%	7.14%	17.86%
Emeritus	53.33%	0.00%	6.67%	6.67%	0.00%	0.00%	33.33%
Other	55.56%	0.00%	0.00%	0.00%	22.22%	0.00%	22.22%

Table 2.1.4 If you use Westlaw Edge, rate the usefulness to you of the following features. Westlaw Answers. Broken out by age of respondent

Age of respondent	No Answer	Essential	Highly Useful	Often Useful	Sometimes Useful	Not really Useful	Not really familiar with this feature
Under 40	33.33%	0.00%	0.00%	0.00%	33.33%	0.00%	33.33%
40-49	57.89%	0.00%	5.26%	5.26%	0.00%	5.26%	26.32%
50-59	30.30%	0.00%	3.03%	6.06%	12.12%	9.09%	39.39%
60 or over	50.67%	0.00%	6.67%	4.00%	8.00%	2.67%	28.00%
Unknown	0.00%	0.00%	0.00%	100.00%	0.00%	0.00%	0.00%

Table 2.1.5 If you use Westlaw Edge, rate the usefulness to you of the following features. Westlaw Answers. Broken out by gender of respondent

Gender of respondent	No Answer	Essential	Highly Useful	Often Useful	Sometimes Useful	Not really Useful	Not really familiar with this feature
Male	47.50%	0.00%	5.00%	3.75%	7.50%	2.50%	33.75%
Female	42.00%	0.00%	6.00%	4.00%	12.00%	8.00%	28.00%
Other	50.00%	0.00%	0.00%	50.00%	0.00%	0.00%	0.00%

Table 2.1.6 If you use Westlaw Edge, rate the usefulness to you of the following features. Westlaw Answers. Broken out by public or private law school

Public or private law school	No Answer	Essential	Highly Useful	Often Useful	Sometimes Useful	Not really Useful	Not really familiar with this feature
Public	46.91%	0.00%	2.47%	4.94%	13.58%	3.70%	28.40%
Private	43.40%	0.00%	9.43%	5.66%	1.89%	5.66%	33.96%

Table 2.1.7 If you use Westlaw Edge, rate the usefulness to you of the following features. Westlaw Answers. Broken out by # of courses taught last semester

# of courses taught last semester	No Answer	Essential	Highly Useful	Often Useful	Sometimes Useful	Not really Useful	Not really familiar with this feature
None	37.04%	0.00%	3.70%	7.41%	11.11%	0.00%	40.74%
One	52.50%	0.00%	0.00%	2.50%	10.00%	12.50%	22.50%
Two	38.98%	0.00%	10.17%	6.78%	8.47%	1.69%	33.90%
More than two	87.50%	0.00%	0.00%	0.00%	0.00%	0.00%	12.50%

Table 2.1.8 If you use Westlaw Edge, rate the usefulness to you of the following features. Westlaw Answers. Broken out by ranking

Ranking	No Answer	Essential	Highly Useful	Often Useful	Sometimes Useful	Not really Useful	Not really familiar with this feature
Top 20 law school	66.67%	0.00%	0.00%	3.70%	11.11%	0.00%	18.52%
Somewhere in the 21-75 rank	36.36%	0.00%	7.27%	5.45%	5.45%	9.09%	36.36%
76 to 250	41.30%	0.00%	6.52%	6.52%	10.87%	2.17%	32.61%
Other	66.67%	0.00%	0.00%	0.00%	16.67%	0.00%	16.67%

Table 2.1.9 If you use Westlaw Edge, rate the usefulness to you of the following features. Westlaw Answers. Broken out by political views

Political views	No Answer	Essential	Highly Useful	Often Useful	Sometimes Useful	Not really Useful	Not really familiar with this feature
Conservative	35.71%	0.00%	0.00%	0.00%	21.43%	0.00%	42.86%
Centrist	44.12%	0.00%	5.88%	8.82%	8.82%	2.94%	29.41%
Liberal	43.08%	0.00%	7.69%	6.15%	6.15%	6.15%	30.77%
Left of Liberal	60.00%	0.00%	0.00%	0.00%	10.00%	5.00%	25.00%
Unknown	100.00%	0.00%	0.00%	0.00%	0.00%	0.00%	0.00%

Table 2.2.1 If you use Westlaw Edge, rate the usefulness to you of the following features. Litigation Analytics.

	No Answer	Essential	Highly Useful	Often Useful	Sometimes Useful	Not really Useful	Not really familiar with this feature
Entire sample	46.27%	0.00%	1.49%	5.97%	7.46%	4.48%	34.33%

Table 2.2.2 If you use Westlaw Edge, rate the usefulness to you of the following features. Litigation Analytics. Broken out by law school enrollment

Law school enrollment	No Answer	Essential	Highly Useful	Often Useful	Sometimes Useful	Not really Useful	Not really familiar with this feature
Less than 400	62.50%	0.00%	0.00%	3.13%	9.38%	3.13%	21.88%
400+ - 550	40.63%	0.00%	0.00%	9.38%	9.38%	6.25%	34.38%
550+ - 800	38.24%	0.00%	5.88%	8.82%	5.88%	8.82%	32.35%
More than 800	44.44%	0.00%	0.00%	2.78%	5.56%	0.00%	47.22%

Table 2.2.3 If you use Westlaw Edge, rate the usefulness to you of the following features. Litigation Analytics. Broken out by academic title

Academic title	No Answer	Essential	Highly Useful	Often Useful	Sometimes Useful	Not really Useful	Not really familiar with this feature
Professor	49.18%	0.00%	1.64%	1.64%	9.84%	4.92%	32.79%
Assistant/ Associate Professor	23.81%	0.00%	0.00%	4.76%	9.52%	4.76%	57.14%
Adjunct/ Clinical Faculty	50.00%	0.00%	0.00%	14.29%	7.14%	7.14%	21.43%
Emeritus	53.33%	0.00%	6.67%	6.67%	0.00%	0.00%	33.33%
Other	55.56%	0.00%	0.00%	11.11%	0.00%	0.00%	33.33%

Table 2.2.4 If you use Westlaw Edge, rate the usefulness to you of the following features. Litigation Analytics. Broken out by age of respondent

Age of respondent	No Answer	Essential	Highly Useful	Often Useful	Sometimes Useful	Not really Useful	Not really familiar with this feature
Under 40	33.33%	0.00%	0.00%	16.67%	0.00%	0.00%	50.00%
40-49	57.89%	0.00%	0.00%	5.26%	10.53%	0.00%	26.32%
50-59	30.30%	0.00%	3.03%	3.03%	18.18%	6.06%	39.39%
60 or over	52.00%	0.00%	1.33%	6.67%	2.67%	5.33%	32.00%
Unknown	0.00%	0.00%	0.00%	0.00%	0.00%	0.00%	100.00%

Table 2.2.5 If you use Westlaw Edge, rate the usefulness to you of the following features. Litigation Analytics. Broken out by gender of respondent

Gender of respondent	No Answer	Essential	Highly Useful	Often Useful	Sometimes Useful	Not really Useful	Not really familiar with this feature
Male	48.75%	0.00%	1.25%	6.25%	6.25%	3.75%	33.75%
Female	42.00%	0.00%	2.00%	4.00%	10.00%	6.00%	36.00%
Other	50.00%	0.00%	0.00%	25.00%	0.00%	0.00%	25.00%

Table 2.2.6 If you use Westlaw Edge, rate the usefulness to you of the following features. Litigation Analytics. Broken out by public or private law school

Public or private law school	No Answer	Essential	Highly Useful	Often Useful	Sometimes Useful	Not really Useful	Not really familiar with this feature
Public	46.91%	0.00%	0.00%	7.41%	7.41%	3.70%	34.57%
Private	45.28%	0.00%	3.77%	3.77%	7.55%	5.66%	33.96%

Table 2.2.7 If you use Westlaw Edge, rate the usefulness to you of the following features. Litigation Analytics. Broken out by # of courses taught last semester

# of courses taught last semester	No Answer	Essential	Highly Useful	Often Useful	Sometimes Useful	Not really Useful	Not really familiar with this feature
None	37.04%	0.00%	3.70%	7.41%	7.41%	3.70%	40.74%
One	52.50%	0.00%	0.00%	7.50%	12.50%	5.00%	22.50%
Two	40.68%	0.00%	1.69%	5.08%	5.08%	5.08%	42.37%
More than two	87.50%	0.00%	0.00%	0.00%	0.00%	0.00%	12.50%

Table 2.2.8 If you use Westlaw Edge, rate the usefulness to you of the following features. Litigation Analytics. Broken out by ranking

Ranking	No Answer	Essential	Highly Useful	Often Useful	Sometimes Useful	Not really Useful	Not really familiar with this feature
Top 20 law school	66.67%	0.00%	0.00%	7.41%	7.41%	0.00%	18.52%
Somewhere in the 21-75 rank	36.36%	0.00%	3.64%	9.09%	7.27%	7.27%	36.36%
76 to 250	43.48%	0.00%	0.00%	2.17%	8.70%	2.17%	43.48%
Other	66.67%	0.00%	0.00%	0.00%	0.00%	16.67%	16.67%

Table 2.2.9 If you use Westlaw Edge, rate the usefulness to you of the following features. Litigation Analytics. Broken out by political views

Political views	No Answer	Essential	Highly Useful	Often Useful	Sometimes Useful	Not really Useful	Not really familiar with this feature
Conservative	35.71%	0.00%	0.00%	0.00%	7.14%	0.00%	57.14%
Centrist	44.12%	0.00%	2.94%	8.82%	8.82%	5.88%	29.41%
Liberal	44.62%	0.00%	1.54%	6.15%	7.69%	4.62%	35.38%
Left of Liberal	60.00%	0.00%	0.00%	5.00%	5.00%	5.00%	25.00%
Unknown	100.00%	0.00%	0.00%	0.00%	0.00%	0.00%	0.00%

Table 2.3.1 If you use Westlaw Edge, rate the usefulness to you of the following features. WestSearch Plus.

	No Answer	Essential	Highly Useful	Often Useful	Sometimes Useful	Not really Useful	Not really familiar with this feature
Entire sample	46.27%	3.73%	4.48%	7.46%	7.46%	0.75%	29.85%

Table 2.3.2 If you use Westlaw Edge, rate the usefulness to you of the following features. WestSearch Plus. Broken out by law school enrollment

Law school enrollment	No Answer	Essential	Highly Useful	Often Useful	Sometimes Useful	Not really Useful	Not really familiar with this feature
Less than 400	59.38%	0.00%	3.13%	6.25%	6.25%	0.00%	25.00%
400+ - 550	40.63%	9.38%	6.25%	6.25%	15.63%	0.00%	21.88%
550+ - 800	41.18%	0.00%	8.82%	14.71%	5.88%	2.94%	26.47%
More than 800	44.44%	5.56%	0.00%	2.78%	2.78%	0.00%	44.44%

Table 2.3.3 If you use Westlaw Edge, rate the usefulness to you of the following features. WestSearch Plus. Broken out by academic title

Academic title	No Answer	Essential	Highly Useful	Often Useful	Sometimes Useful	Not really Useful	Not really familiar with this feature
Professor	47.54%	4.92%	6.56%	6.56%	8.20%	0.00%	26.23%
Assistant/ Associate Professor	23.81%	4.76%	4.76%	0.00%	14.29%	0.00%	52.38%
Adjunct/ Clinical Faculty	50.00%	3.57%	0.00%	17.86%	7.14%	3.57%	17.86%
Emeritus	60.00%	0.00%	6.67%	0.00%	0.00%	0.00%	33.33%
Other	55.56%	0.00%	0.00%	11.11%	0.00%	0.00%	33.33%

Table 2.3.4 If you use Westlaw Edge, rate the usefulness to you of the following features. WestSearch Plus. Broken out by age of respondent

Age of respondent	No Answer	Essential	Highly Useful	Often Useful	Sometimes Useful	Not really Useful	Not really familiar with this feature
Under 40	33.33%	0.00%	16.67%	0.00%	16.67%	0.00%	33.33%
40-49	57.89%	5.26%	0.00%	5.26%	5.26%	0.00%	26.32%
50-59	30.30%	3.03%	6.06%	6.06%	12.12%	3.03%	39.39%
60 or over	52.00%	4.00%	4.00%	9.33%	5.33%	0.00%	25.33%
Unknown	0.00%	0.00%	0.00%	0.00%	0.00%	0.00%	100.00%

Table 2.3.5 If you use Westlaw Edge, rate the usefulness to you of the following features. WestSearch Plus. Broken out by gender of respondent

Gender of respondent	No Answer	Essential	Highly Useful	Often Useful	Sometimes Useful	Not really Useful	Not really familiar with this feature
Male	48.75%	5.00%	3.75%	6.25%	6.25%	1.25%	28.75%
Female	42.00%	2.00%	6.00%	8.00%	10.00%	0.00%	32.00%
Other	50.00%	0.00%	0.00%	25.00%	0.00%	0.00%	25.00%

Table 2.3.6 If you use Westlaw Edge, rate the usefulness to you of the following features. WestSearch Plus. Broken out by public or private law school

Public or private law school	No Answer	Essential	Highly Useful	Often Useful	Sometimes Useful	Not really Useful	Not really familiar with this feature
Public	46.91%	3.70%	2.47%	8.64%	8.64%	1.23%	28.40%
Private	45.28%	3.77%	7.55%	5.66%	5.66%	0.00%	32.08%

Table 2.3.7 If you use Westlaw Edge, rate the usefulness to you of the following features. WestSearch Plus. Broken out by # of courses taught last semester

# of courses taught last semester	No Answer	Essential	Highly Useful	Often Useful	Sometimes Useful	Not really Useful	Not really familiar with this feature
None	40.74%	0.00%	3.70%	11.11%	3.70%	0.00%	40.74%
One	52.50%	2.50%	2.50%	10.00%	10.00%	2.50%	20.00%
Two	38.98%	6.78%	6.78%	3.39%	8.47%	0.00%	35.59%
More than two	87.50%	0.00%	0.00%	12.50%	0.00%	0.00%	0.00%

Table 2.3.8 If you use Westlaw Edge, rate the usefulness to you of the following features. WestSearch Plus. Broken out by ranking

Ranking	No Answer	Essential	Highly Useful	Often Useful	Sometimes Useful	Not really Useful	Not really familiar with this feature
Top 20 law school	66.67%	3.70%	0.00%	7.41%	3.70%	0.00%	18.52%
Somewhere in the 21-75 rank	38.18%	1.82%	7.27%	9.09%	7.27%	1.82%	34.55%
76 to 250	41.30%	6.52%	4.35%	6.52%	8.70%	0.00%	32.61%
Other	66.67%	0.00%	0.00%	0.00%	16.67%	0.00%	16.67%

Table 2.3.9 If you use Westlaw Edge, rate the usefulness to you of the following features. WestSearch Plus. Broken out by political views

Political views	No Answer	Essential	Highly Useful	Often Useful	Sometimes Useful	Not really Useful	Not really familiar with this feature
Conservative	35.71%	7.14%	0.00%	7.14%	7.14%	0.00%	42.86%
Centrist	47.06%	5.88%	2.94%	5.88%	11.76%	2.94%	23.53%
Liberal	43.08%	3.08%	7.69%	7.69%	6.15%	0.00%	32.31%
Left of Liberal	60.00%	0.00%	0.00%	10.00%	5.00%	0.00%	25.00%
Unknown	100.00%	0.00%	0.00%	0.00%	0.00%	0.00%	0.00%

Table 2.4.1 If you use Westlaw Edge, rate the usefulness to you of the following features. Statutes or Regulations Compare.

	No Answer	Essential	Highly Useful	Often Useful	Sometimes Useful	Not really Useful	Not really familiar with this feature
Entire sample	47.01%	0.75%	4.48%	5.97%	5.22%	0.75%	35.82%

Table 2.4.2 If you use Westlaw Edge, rate the usefulness to you of the following features. Statutes or Regulations Compare. Broken out by law school enrollment

Law school enrollment	No Answer	Essential	Highly Useful	Often Useful	Sometimes Useful	Not really Useful	Not really familiar with this feature
Less than 400	62.50%	0.00%	0.00%	6.25%	6.25%	0.00%	25.00%
400+ - 550	40.63%	0.00%	9.38%	9.38%	0.00%	3.13%	37.50%
550+ - 800	41.18%	0.00%	8.82%	5.88%	8.82%	0.00%	35.29%
More than 800	44.44%	2.78%	0.00%	2.78%	5.56%	0.00%	44.44%

Table 2.4.3 If you use Westlaw Edge, rate the usefulness to you of the following features. Statutes or Regulations Compare. Broken out by academic title

Academic title	No Answer	Essential	Highly Useful	Often Useful	Sometimes Useful	Not really Useful	Not really familiar with this feature
Professor	49.18%	1.64%	4.92%	4.92%	4.92%	0.00%	34.43%
Assistant/ Associate Professor	23.81%	0.00%	4.76%	9.52%	4.76%	0.00%	57.14%
Adjunct/ Clinical Faculty	50.00%	0.00%	7.14%	10.71%	7.14%	3.57%	21.43%
Emeritus	60.00%	0.00%	0.00%	0.00%	6.67%	0.00%	33.33%
Other	55.56%	0.00%	0.00%	0.00%	0.00%	0.00%	44.44%

Table 2.4.4 If you use Westlaw Edge, rate the usefulness to you of the following features. Statutes or Regulations Compare. Broken out by age of respondent

Age of respondent	No Answer	Essential	Highly Useful	Often Useful	Sometimes Useful	Not really Useful	Not really familiar with this feature
Under 40	33.33%	0.00%	0.00%	16.67%	16.67%	0.00%	33.33%
40-49	57.89%	0.00%	5.26%	10.53%	0.00%	0.00%	26.32%
50-59	30.30%	0.00%	12.12%	3.03%	6.06%	0.00%	48.48%
60 or over	53.33%	1.33%	1.33%	5.33%	5.33%	1.33%	32.00%
Unknown	0.00%	0.00%	0.00%	0.00%	0.00%	0.00%	100.00%

Table 2.4.5 If you use Westlaw Edge, rate the usefulness to you of the following features. Statutes or Regulations Compare. Broken out by gender of respondent

Gender of respondent	No Answer	Essential	Highly Useful	Often Useful	Sometimes Useful	Not really Useful	Not really familiar with this feature
Male	50.00%	1.25%	3.75%	1.25%	6.25%	1.25%	36.25%
Female	42.00%	0.00%	6.00%	12.00%	4.00%	0.00%	36.00%
Other	50.00%	0.00%	0.00%	25.00%	0.00%	0.00%	25.00%

Table 2.4.6 If you use Westlaw Edge, rate the usefulness to you of the following features. Statutes or Regulations Compare. Broken out by public or private law school

Public or private law school	No Answer	Essential	Highly Useful	Often Useful	Sometimes Useful	Not really Useful	Not really familiar with this feature
Public	46.91%	1.23%	3.70%	8.64%	6.17%	1.23%	32.10%
Private	47.17%	0.00%	5.66%	1.89%	3.77%	0.00%	41.51%

Table 2.4.7 If you use Westlaw Edge, rate the usefulness to you of the following features. Statutes or Regulations Compare. Broken out by # of courses taught last semester

# of courses taught last semester	No Answer	Essential	Highly Useful	Often Useful	Sometimes Useful	Not really Useful	Not really familiar with this feature
None	40.74%	0.00%	0.00%	7.41%	11.11%	0.00%	40.74%
One	52.50%	2.50%	5.00%	5.00%	2.50%	0.00%	32.50%
Two	40.68%	0.00%	6.78%	6.78%	5.08%	1.69%	38.98%
More than two	87.50%	0.00%	0.00%	0.00%	0.00%	0.00%	12.50%

Table 2.4.8 If you use Westlaw Edge, rate the usefulness to you of the following features. Statutes or Regulations Compare. Broken out by ranking

Ranking	No Answer	Essential	Highly Useful	Often Useful	Sometimes Useful	Not really Useful	Not really familiar with this feature
Top 20 law school	66.67%	3.70%	3.70%	3.70%	3.70%	0.00%	18.52%
Somewhere in the 21-75 rank	38.18%	0.00%	5.45%	9.09%	3.64%	1.82%	41.82%
76 to 250	43.48%	0.00%	4.35%	4.35%	6.52%	0.00%	41.30%
Other	66.67%	0.00%	0.00%	0.00%	16.67%	0.00%	16.67%

Table 2.4.9 If you use Westlaw Edge, rate the usefulness to you of the following features. Statutes or Regulations Compare. Broken out by political views

Political views	No Answer	Essential	Highly Useful	Often Useful	Sometimes Useful	Not really Useful	Not really familiar with this feature
Conservative	35.71%	7.14%	0.00%	0.00%	7.14%	0.00%	50.00%
Centrist	47.06%	0.00%	5.88%	5.88%	11.76%	0.00%	29.41%
Liberal	44.62%	0.00%	6.15%	7.69%	1.54%	1.54%	38.46%
Left of Liberal	60.00%	0.00%	0.00%	5.00%	5.00%	0.00%	30.00%
Unknown	100.00%	0.00%	0.00%	0.00%	0.00%	0.00%	0.00%

Table 2.5.1 If you use Westlaw Edge, rate the usefulness to you of the following features. KeyCite Overruling Risk.

	No Answer	Essential	Highly Useful	Often Useful	Sometimes Useful	Not really Useful	Not really familiar with this feature
Entire sample	47.01%	4.48%	4.48%	2.99%	6.72%	2.24%	32.09%

Table 2.5.2 If you use Westlaw Edge, rate the usefulness to you of the following features. KeyCite Overruling Risk. Broken out by law school enrollment

Law school enrollment	No Answer	Essential	Highly Useful	Often Useful	Sometimes Useful	Not really Useful	Not really familiar with this feature
Less than 400	62.50%	3.13%	3.13%	0.00%	6.25%	0.00%	25.00%
400+ - 550	40.63%	9.38%	9.38%	0.00%	6.25%	6.25%	28.13%
550+ - 800	41.18%	2.94%	5.88%	11.76%	8.82%	0.00%	29.41%
More than 800	44.44%	2.78%	0.00%	0.00%	5.56%	2.78%	44.44%

Table 2.5.3 If you use Westlaw Edge, rate the usefulness to you of the following features. KeyCite Overruling Risk. Broken out by academic title

Academic title	No Answer	Essential	Highly Useful	Often Useful	Sometimes Useful	Not really Useful	Not really familiar with this feature
Professor	49.18%	3.28%	1.64%	4.92%	8.20%	1.64%	31.15%
Assistant/ Associate Professor	23.81%	9.52%	9.52%	0.00%	9.52%	4.76%	42.86%
Adjunct/ Clinical Faculty	50.00%	7.14%	7.14%	3.57%	7.14%	3.57%	21.43%
Emeritus	60.00%	0.00%	6.67%	0.00%	0.00%	0.00%	33.33%
Other	55.56%	0.00%	0.00%	0.00%	0.00%	0.00%	44.44%

Table 2.5.4 If you use Westlaw Edge, rate the usefulness to you of the following features. KeyCite Overruling Risk. Broken out by age of respondent

Age of respondent	No Answer	Essential	Highly Useful	Often Useful	Sometimes Useful	Not really Useful	Not really familiar with this feature
Under 40	33.33%	0.00%	0.00%	0.00%	33.33%	0.00%	33.33%
40-49	57.89%	0.00%	15.79%	0.00%	0.00%	5.26%	21.05%
50-59	30.30%	12.12%	3.03%	3.03%	15.15%	3.03%	33.33%
60 or over	53.33%	2.67%	2.67%	4.00%	2.67%	1.33%	33.33%
Unknown	0.00%	0.00%	0.00%	0.00%	0.00%	0.00%	100.00%

Table 2.5.5 If you use Westlaw Edge, rate the usefulness to you of the following features. KeyCite Overruling Risk. Broken out by gender of respondent

Gender of respondent	No Answer	Essential	Highly Useful	Often Useful	Sometimes Useful	Not really Useful	Not really familiar with this feature
Male	50.00%	3.75%	3.75%	3.75%	3.75%	1.25%	33.75%
Female	42.00%	6.00%	6.00%	2.00%	12.00%	4.00%	28.00%
Other	50.00%	0.00%	0.00%	0.00%	0.00%	0.00%	50.00%

Table 2.5.6 If you use Westlaw Edge, rate the usefulness to you of the following features. KeyCite Overruling Risk. Broken out by public or private law school

Public or private law school	No Answer	Essential	Highly Useful	Often Useful	Sometimes Useful	Not really Useful	Not really familiar with this feature
Public	46.91%	6.17%	4.94%	3.70%	7.41%	2.47%	28.40%
Private	47.17%	1.89%	3.77%	1.89%	5.66%	1.89%	37.74%

Table 2.5.7 If you use Westlaw Edge, rate the usefulness to you of the following features. KeyCite Overruling Risk. Broken out by # of courses taught last semester

# of courses taught last semester	No Answer	Essential	Highly Useful	Often Useful	Sometimes Useful	Not really Useful	Not really familiar with this feature
None	40.74%	3.70%	7.41%	0.00%	3.70%	0.00%	44.44%
One	52.50%	2.50%	5.00%	2.50%	7.50%	2.50%	27.50%
Two	40.68%	6.78%	3.39%	3.39%	8.47%	3.39%	33.90%
More than two	87.50%	0.00%	0.00%	12.50%	0.00%	0.00%	0.00%

Table 2.5.8 If you use Westlaw Edge, rate the usefulness to you of the following features. KeyCite Overruling Risk. Broken out by ranking

Ranking	No Answer	Essential	Highly Useful	Often Useful	Sometimes Useful	Not really Useful	Not really familiar with this feature
Top 20 law school	66.67%	3.70%	0.00%	0.00%	7.41%	0.00%	22.22%
Somewhere in the 21-75 rank	38.18%	3.64%	7.27%	5.45%	3.64%	3.64%	38.18%
76 to 250	43.48%	6.52%	4.35%	2.17%	8.70%	2.17%	32.61%
Other	66.67%	0.00%	0.00%	0.00%	16.67%	0.00%	16.67%

Table 2.5.9 If you use Westlaw Edge, rate the usefulness to you of the following features. KeyCite Overruling Risk. Broken out by political views

Political views	No Answer	Essential	Highly Useful	Often Useful	Sometimes Useful	Not really Useful	Not really familiar with this feature
Conservative	35.71%	7.14%	0.00%	0.00%	7.14%	0.00%	50.00%
Centrist	47.06%	8.82%	0.00%	5.88%	8.82%	0.00%	29.41%
Liberal	44.62%	1.54%	3.08%	3.08%	7.69%	3.08%	36.92%
Left of Liberal	60.00%	5.00%	20.00%	0.00%	0.00%	5.00%	10.00%
Unknown	100.00%	0.00%	0.00%	0.00%	0.00%	0.00%	0.00%

Table 2.6.1 If you use Westlaw Edge, rate the usefulness to you of the following features. Brief Analysis.

	No Answer	Essential	Highly Useful	Often Useful	Sometimes Useful	Not really Useful	Not really familiar with this feature
Entire sample	47.76%	1.49%	2.99%	3.73%	3.73%	2.99%	37.31%

Table 2.6.2 If you use Westlaw Edge, rate the usefulness to you of the following features. Brief Analysis. Broken out by law school enrollment

Law school enrollment	No Answer	Essential	Highly Useful	Often Useful	Sometimes Useful	Not really Useful	Not really familiar with this feature
Less than 400	59.38%	0.00%	6.25%	0.00%	0.00%	3.13%	31.25%
400+ - 550	40.63%	0.00%	0.00%	6.25%	9.38%	6.25%	37.50%
550+ - 800	44.12%	0.00%	5.88%	5.88%	2.94%	2.94%	38.24%
More than 800	47.22%	5.56%	0.00%	2.78%	2.78%	0.00%	41.67%

Table 2.6.3 If you use Westlaw Edge, rate the usefulness to you of the following features. Brief Analysis. Broken out by academic title

Academic title	No Answer	Essential	Highly Useful	Often Useful	Sometimes Useful	Not really Useful	Not really familiar with this feature
Professor	49.18%	1.64%	4.92%	3.28%	3.28%	1.64%	36.07%
Assistant/ Associate Professor	23.81%	4.76%	0.00%	4.76%	9.52%	4.76%	52.38%
Adjunct/ Clinical Faculty	53.57%	0.00%	3.57%	3.57%	3.57%	7.14%	28.57%
Emeritus	60.00%	0.00%	0.00%	6.67%	0.00%	0.00%	33.33%
Other	55.56%	0.00%	0.00%	0.00%	0.00%	0.00%	44.44%

Table 2.6.4 If you use Westlaw Edge, rate the usefulness to you of the following features. Brief Analysis. Broken out by age of respondent

Age of respondent	No Answer	Essential	Highly Useful	Often Useful	Sometimes Useful	Not really Useful	Not really familiar with this feature
Under 40	33.33%	0.00%	0.00%	0.00%	16.67%	0.00%	50.00%
40-49	57.89%	0.00%	0.00%	0.00%	5.26%	5.26%	31.58%
50-59	30.30%	3.03%	9.09%	3.03%	6.06%	3.03%	45.45%
60 or over	54.67%	1.33%	1.33%	5.33%	1.33%	2.67%	33.33%
Unknown	0.00%	0.00%	0.00%	0.00%	0.00%	0.00%	100.00%

Table 2.6.5 If you use Westlaw Edge, rate the usefulness to you of the following features. Brief Analysis. Broken out by gender of respondent

Gender of respondent	No Answer	Essential	Highly Useful	Often Useful	Sometimes Useful	Not really Useful	Not really familiar with this feature
Male	50.00%	0.00%	1.25%	6.25%	2.50%	2.50%	37.50%
Female	44.00%	4.00%	6.00%	0.00%	6.00%	4.00%	36.00%
Other	50.00%	0.00%	0.00%	0.00%	0.00%	0.00%	50.00%

Table 2.6.6 If you use Westlaw Edge, rate the usefulness to you of the following features. Brief Analysis. Broken out by public or private law school

Public or private law school	No Answer	Essential	Highly Useful	Often Useful	Sometimes Useful	Not really Useful	Not really familiar with this feature
Public	46.91%	1.23%	1.23%	4.94%	4.94%	3.70%	37.04%
Private	49.06%	1.89%	5.66%	1.89%	1.89%	1.89%	37.74%

Table 2.6.7 If you use Westlaw Edge, rate the usefulness to you of the following features. Brief Analysis. Broken out by # of courses taught last semester

# of courses taught last semester	No Answer	Essential	Highly Useful	Often Useful	Sometimes Useful	Not really Useful	Not really familiar with this feature
None	44.44%	0.00%	3.70%	3.70%	3.70%	0.00%	44.44%
One	55.00%	0.00%	2.50%	2.50%	5.00%	5.00%	30.00%
Two	38.98%	3.39%	3.39%	5.08%	3.39%	3.39%	42.37%
More than two	87.50%	0.00%	0.00%	0.00%	0.00%	0.00%	12.50%

Table 2.6.8 If you use Westlaw Edge, rate the usefulness to you of the following features. Brief Analysis. Broken out by ranking

Ranking	No Answer	Essential	Highly Useful	Often Useful	Sometimes Useful	Not really Useful	Not really familiar with this feature
Top 20 law school	70.37%	0.00%	0.00%	3.70%	3.70%	3.70%	18.52%
Somewhere in the 21-75 rank	40.00%	0.00%	3.64%	5.45%	1.82%	3.64%	45.45%
76 to 250	41.30%	4.35%	4.35%	2.17%	6.52%	0.00%	41.30%
Other	66.67%	0.00%	0.00%	0.00%	0.00%	16.67%	16.67%

Table 2.6.9 If you use Westlaw Edge, rate the usefulness to you of the following features. Brief Analysis. Broken out by political views

Political views	No Answer	Essential	Highly Useful	Often Useful	Sometimes Useful	Not really Useful	Not really familiar with this feature
Conservative	35.71%	0.00%	0.00%	7.14%	7.14%	0.00%	50.00%
Centrist	47.06%	0.00%	2.94%	8.82%	2.94%	2.94%	35.29%
Liberal	46.15%	3.08%	4.62%	1.54%	3.08%	3.08%	38.46%
Left of Liberal	60.00%	0.00%	0.00%	0.00%	5.00%	5.00%	30.00%
Unknown	100.00%	0.00%	0.00%	0.00%	0.00%	0.00%	0.00%

Table 2.7.1 If you use Westlaw Edge, rate the usefulness to you of the following features. Contract Review.

	No Answer	Essential	Highly Useful	Often Useful	Sometimes Useful	Not really Useful	Not really familiar with this feature
Entire sample	47.76%	0.00%	0.75%	1.49%	3.73%	1.49%	44.78%

Table 2.7.2 If you use Westlaw Edge, rate the usefulness to you of the following features. Contract Review. Broken out by law school enrollment

Law school enrollment	No Answer	Essential	Highly Useful	Often Useful	Sometimes Useful	Not really Useful	Not really familiar with this feature
Less than 400	59.38%	0.00%	3.13%	0.00%	3.13%	0.00%	34.38%
400+ - 550	40.63%	0.00%	0.00%	0.00%	6.25%	6.25%	46.88%
550+ - 800	41.18%	0.00%	0.00%	5.88%	2.94%	0.00%	50.00%
More than 800	50.00%	0.005	0.00%	0.00%	2.78%	0.00%	47.22%

Table 2.7.3 If you use Westlaw Edge, rate the usefulness to you of the following features. Contract Review. Broken out by academic title

Academic title	No Answer	Essential	Highly Useful	Often Useful	Sometimes Useful	Not really Useful	Not really familiar with this feature
Professor	49.18%	0.00%	1.64%	1.64%	1.64%	0.00%	45.90%
Assistant/ Associate Professor	23.81%	0.00%	0.00%	0.00%	4.76%	4.76%	66.67%
Adjunct/ Clinical Faculty	53.57%	0.00%	0.00%	0.00%	7.14%	3.57%	35.71%
Emeritus	60.00%	0.00%	0.00%	6.67%	0.00%	0.00%	33.33%
Other	55.56%	0.00%	0.00%	0.00%	11.11%	0.00%	33.33%

Table 2.7.4 If you use Westlaw Edge, rate the usefulness to you of the following features. Contract Review. Broken out by age of respondent

Age of respondent	No Answer	Essential	Highly Useful	Often Useful	Sometimes Useful	Not really Useful	Not really familiar with this feature
Under 40	33.33%	0.00%	0.00%	0.00%	16.67%	0.00%	50.00%
40-49	57.89%	0.00%	0.00%	0.00%	0.00%	5.26%	36.84%
50-59	30.30%	0.00%	0.00%	0.00%	3.03%	0.00%	66.67%
60 or over	54.67%	0.00%	1.33%	2.67%	4.00%	1.33%	36.00%
Unknown	0.00%	0.00%	0.00%	0.00%	0.00%	0.00%	100.00%

Table 2.7.5 If you use Westlaw Edge, rate the usefulness to you of the following features. Contract Review. Broken out by gender of respondent

Gender of respondent	No Answer	Essential	Highly Useful	Often Useful	Sometimes Useful	Not really Useful	Not really familiar with this feature
Male	51.25%	0.00%	1.25%	2.50%	1.25%	1.25%	42.50%
Female	42.00%	0.00%	0.00%	0.00%	8.00%	2.00%	48.00%
Other	50.00%	0.00%	0.00%	0.00%	0.00%	0.00%	50.00%

Table 2.7.6 If you use Westlaw Edge, rate the usefulness to you of the following features. Contract Review. Broken out by public or private law school

Public or private law school	No Answer	Essential	Highly Useful	Often Useful	Sometimes Useful	Not really Useful	Not really familiar with this feature
Public	48.15%	0.00%	0.00%	1.23%	6.17%	2.47%	41.98%
Private	47.17%	0.00%	1.89%	1.89%	0.00%	0.00%	49.06%

Table 2.7.7 If you use Westlaw Edge, rate the usefulness to you of the following features. Contract Review. Broken out by # of courses taught last semester

# of courses taught last semester	No Answer	Essential	Highly Useful	Often Useful	Sometimes Useful	Not really Useful	Not really familiar with this feature
None	44.44%	0.00%	0.00%	3.70%	3.70%	0.00%	48.15%
One	55.00%	0.00%	0.00%	0.00%	2.50%	2.50%	40.00%
Two	38.98%	0.00%	1.69%	1.69%	5.08%	1.69%	50.85%
More than two	87.50%	0.00%	0.00%	0.00%	0.00%	0.00%	12.50%

Table 2.7.8 If you use Westlaw Edge, rate the usefulness to you of the following features. Contract Review. Broken out by ranking

Ranking	No Answer	Essential	Highly Useful	Often Useful	Sometimes Useful	Not really Useful	Not really familiar with this feature
Top 20 law school	74.07%	0.00%	0.00%	0.00%	3.70%	0.00%	22.22%
Somewhere in the 21-75 rank	38.18%	0.00%	0.00%	3.64%	3.64%	3.64%	50.91%
76 to 250	41.30%	0.00%	2.17%	0.00%	4.35%	0.00%	52.17%
Other	66.67%	0.00%	0.00%	0.00%	0.00%	0.00%	33.33%

Table 2.7.9 If you use Westlaw Edge, rate the usefulness to you of the following features. Contract Review. Broken out by political views

Political views	No Answer	Essential	Highly Useful	Often Useful	Sometimes Useful	Not really Useful	Not really familiar with this feature
Conservative	42.86%	0.00%	0.00%	0.00%	0.00%	0.00%	57.14%
Centrist	47.06%	0.00%	0.00%	2.94%	8.82%	0.00%	41.18%
Liberal	44.62%	0.00%	1.54%	1.54%	3.08%	1.54%	47.69%
Left of Liberal	60.00%	0.00%	0.00%	0.00%	0.00%	5.00%	35.00%
Unknown	100.00%	0.00%	0.00%	0.00%	0.00%	0.00%	0.00%

Table 3 If you use Lexis+, rate the usefulness to you of the following features:

Table 3.1.1 If you use Lexis+, rate the usefulness to you of the following features: Les Machina.

	No Answer	Essential	Highly Useful	Often Useful	Sometimes Useful	Not really Useful	Not really familiar with this feature
Entire sample	61.94%	0.00%	0.00%	1.49%	2.24%	1.49%	32.84%

Table 3.1.2 If you use Lexis+, rate the usefulness to you of the following features: Les Machina. Broken out by law school enrollment

Law school enrollment	No Answer	Essential	Highly Useful	Often Useful	Sometimes Useful	Not really Useful	Not really familiar with this feature
Less than 400	71.88%	0.00%	0.00%	0.00%	3.13%	3.13%	21.88%
400+ - 550	59.38%	0.00%	0.00%	0.00%	3.13%	3.13%	34.38%
550+ - 800	52.94%	0.00%	0.00%	5.88%	0.00%	0.00%	41.18%
More than 800	63.89%	0.00%	0.00%	0.00%	2.78%	0.00%	33.33%

Table 3.1.3 If you use Lexis+, rate the usefulness to you of the following features: Les Machina. Broken out by academic title

Academic title	No Answer	Essential	Highly Useful	Often Useful	Sometimes Useful	Not really Useful	Not really familiar with this feature
Professor	73.77%	0.00%	0.00%	0.00%	1.64%	0.00%	24.59%
Assistant/ Associate Professor	38.10%	0.00%	0.00%	0.00%	4.76%	4.76%	52.38%
Adjunct/ Clinical Faculty	57.14%	0.00%	0.00%	3.57%	3.57%	0.00%	35.71%
Emeritus	60.00%	0.00%	0.00%	6.67%	0.00%	0.00%	33.33%
Other	55.56%	0.00%	0.00%	0.00%	0.00%	11.11%	33.33%

Table 3.1.4 If you use Lexis+, rate the usefulness to you of the following features: Les Machina. Broken out by age of respondent

Age of respondent	No Answer	Essential	Highly Useful	Often Useful	Sometimes Useful	Not really Useful	Not really familiar with this feature
Under 40	33.33%	0.00%	0.00%	0.00%	0.00%	0.00%	66.67%
40-49	68.42%	0.00%	0.00%	0.00%	0.00%	5.26%	26.32%
50-59	54.55%	0.00%	0.00%	3.03%	3.03%	0.00%	39.39%
60 or over	65.33%	0.00%	0.00%	1.33%	2.67%	1.33%	29.33%
Unknown	100.00%	0.00%	0.00%	0.00%	0.00%	0.00%	0.00%

Table 3.1.5 If you use Lexis+, rate the usefulness to you of the following features: Les Machina. Broken out by gender of respondent

Gender of respondent	No Answer	Essential	Highly Useful	Often Useful	Sometimes Useful	Not really Useful	Not really familiar with this feature
Male	60.00%	0.00%	0.00%	1.25%	3.75%	0.00%	35.00%
Female	62.00%	0.00%	0.00%	2.00%	0.00%	4.00%	32.00%
Other	100.00%	0.00%	0.00%	0.00%	0.00%	0.00%	0.00%

Table 3.1.6 If you use Lexis+, rate the usefulness to you of the following features: Les Machina. Broken out by public or private law school

Public or private law school	No Answer	Essential	Highly Useful	Often Useful	Sometimes Useful	Not really Useful	Not really familiar with this feature
Public	60.49%	0.00%	0.00%	1.23%	1.23%	2.47%	34.57%
Private	64.15%	0.00%	0.00%	1.89%	3.77%	0.00%	30.19%

Table 3.1.7 If you use Lexis+, rate the usefulness to you of the following features: Les Machina. Broken out by # of courses taught last semester

# of courses taught last semester	No Answer	Essential	Highly Useful	Often Useful	Sometimes Useful	Not really Useful	Not really familiar with this feature
None	48.15%	0.00%	0.00%	3.70%	0.00%	0.00%	48.15%
One	67.50%	0.00%	0.00%	2.50%	0.00%	2.50%	27.50%
Two	61.02%	0.00%	0.00%	0.00%	5.08%	1.69%	32.20%
More than two	87.50%	0.00%	0.00%	0.00%	0.00%	0.00%	12.50%

Table 3.1.8 If you use Lexis+, rate the usefulness to you of the following features: Les Machina. Broken out by ranking

Ranking	No Answer	Essential	Highly Useful	Often Useful	Sometimes Useful	Not really Useful	Not really familiar with this feature
Top 20 law school	77.78%	0.00%	0.00%	3.70%	0.00%	0.00%	18.52%
Somewhere in the 21-75 rank	49.09%	0.00%	0.00%	1.82%	3.64%	1.82%	43.64%
76 to 250	63.04%	0.00%	0.00%	0.00%	2.17%	2.17%	32.61%
Other	100.00%	0.00%	0.00%	0.00%	0.00%	0.00%	0.00%

Table 3.1.9 If you use Lexis+, rate the usefulness to you of the following features: Les Machina. Broken out by political views

Political views	No Answer	Essential	Highly Useful	Often Useful	Sometimes Useful	Not really Useful	Not really familiar with this feature
Conservative	71.43%	0.00%	0.00%	0.00%	7.14%	0.00%	21.43%
Centrist	64.71%	0.00%	0.00%	2.94%	2.94%	0.00%	29.41%
Liberal	58.46%	0.00%	0.00%	1.54%	1.54%	1.54%	36.92%
Left of Liberal	60.00%	0.00%	0.00%	0.00%	0.00%	5.00%	35.00%
Unknown	100.00%	0.00%	0.00%	0.00%	0.00%	0.00%	0.00%

Table 3.2.1 If you use Lexis+, rate the usefulness to you of the following features: Judicial Analytics.

	No Answer	Essential	Highly Useful	Often Useful	Sometimes Useful	Not really Useful	Not really familiar with this feature
Entire sample	61.94%	0.00%	0.75%	2.24%	2.99%	2.99%	29.10%

Table 3.2.2 If you use Lexis+, rate the usefulness to you of the following features: Judicial Analytics. Broken out by law school enrollment

Law school enrollment	No Answer	Essential	Highly Useful	Often Useful	Sometimes Useful	Not really Useful	Not really familiar with this feature
Less than 400	71.88%	0.00%	0.00%	0.00%	3.13%	6.25%	18.75%
400+ - 550	59.38%	0.00%	0.00%	3.13%	6.25%	3.13%	28.13%
550+ - 800	55.88%	0.00%	0.00%	5.88%	0.00%	2.94%	35.29%
More than 800	61.11%	0.00%	2.78%	0.00%	2.78%	0.00%	33.33%

Table 3.2.3 If you use Lexis+, rate the usefulness to you of the following features: Judicial Analytics. Broken out by academic title

Academic title	No Answer	Essential	Highly Useful	Often Useful	Sometimes Useful	Not really Useful	Not really familiar with this feature
Professor	73.77%	0.00%	1.64%	0.00%	3.28%	0.00%	21.31%
Assistant/ Associate Professor	33.33%	0.00%	0.00%	4.76%	9.52%	4.76%	47.62%
Adjunct/ Clinical Faculty	57.14%	0.00%	0.00%	7.14%	0.00%	7.14%	28.57%
Emeritus	66.67%	0.00%	0.00%	0.00%	0.00%	0.00%	33.33%
Other	55.56%	0.00%	0.00%	0.00%	0.00%	11.11%	33.33%

Table 3.2.4 If you use Lexis+, rate the usefulness to you of the following features: Judicial Analytics. Broken out by age of respondent

Age of respondent	No Answer	Essential	Highly Useful	Often Useful	Sometimes Useful	Not really Useful	Not really familiar with this feature
Under 40	33.33%	0.00%	0.00%	16.67%	16.67%	0.00%	33.33%
40-49	68.42%	0.00%	5.26%	5.26%	0.00%	0.00%	21.05%
50-59	51.52%	0.00%	0.00%	3.03%	9.09%	3.03%	33.33%
60 or over	66.67%	0.00%	0.00%	0.00%	0.00%	4.00%	29.33%
Unknown	100.00%	0.00%	0.00%	0.00%	0.00%	0.00%	0.00%

Table 3.2.5 If you use Lexis+, rate the usefulness to you of the following features: Judicial Analytics. Broken out by gender of respondent

Gender of respondent	No Answer	Essential	Highly Useful	Often Useful	Sometimes Useful	Not really Useful	Not really familiar with this feature
Male	61.25%	0.00%	0.00%	0.00%	2.50%	3.75%	32.50%
Female	60.00%	0.00%	2.00%	6.00%	4.00%	2.00%	26.00%
Other	100.00%	0.00%	0.00%	0.00%	0.00%	0.00%	0.00%

Table 3.2.6 If you use Lexis+, rate the usefulness to you of the following features: Judicial Analytics. Broken out by public or private law school

Public or private law school	No Answer	Essential	Highly Useful	Often Useful	Sometimes Useful	Not really Useful	Not really familiar with this feature
Public	59.26%	0.00%	0.00%	3.70%	3.70%	3.70%	29.63%
Private	66.04%	0.00%	1.89%	0.00%	1.89%	1.89%	28.30%

Table 3.2.7 If you use Lexis+, rate the usefulness to you of the following features: Judicial Analytics. Broken out by # of courses taught last semester

# of courses taught last semester	No Answer	Essential	Highly Useful	Often Useful	Sometimes Useful	Not really Useful	Not really familiar with this feature
None	48.15%	0.00%	0.00%	0.00%	3.70%	3.70%	44.44%
One	67.50%	0.00%	2.50%	7.50%	0.00%	0.00%	22.50%
Two	61.02%	0.00%	0.00%	0.00%	5.08%	5.08%	28.81%
More than two	87.50%	0.00%	0.00%	0.00%	0.00%	0.00%	12.50%

Table 3.2.8 If you use Lexis+, rate the usefulness to you of the following features: Judicial Analytics. Broken out by ranking

Ranking	No Answer	Essential	Highly Useful	Often Useful	Sometimes Useful	Not really Useful	Not really familiar with this feature
Top 20 law school	77.78%	0.00%	0.00%	7.41%	0.00%	0.00%	14.81%
Somewhere in the 21-75 rank	50.91%	0.00%	1.82%	1.82%	1.82%	3.64%	40.00%
76 to 250	60.87%	0.00%	0.00%	0.00%	6.52%	4.35%	28.26%
Other	100.00%	0.00%	0.00%	0.00%	0.00%	0.00%	0.00%

Table 3.2.9 If you use Lexis+, rate the usefulness to you of the following features: Judicial Analytics. Broken out by political views

Political views	No Answer	Essential	Highly Useful	Often Useful	Sometimes Useful	Not really Useful	Not really familiar with this feature
Conservative	71.43%	0.00%	0.00%	0.00%	0.00%	0.00%	28.57%
Centrist	64.71%	0.00%	0.00%	0.00%	5.88%	2.94%	26.47%
Liberal	58.46%	0.00%	1.54%	3.08%	3.08%	3.08%	30.77%
Left of Liberal	60.00%	0.00%	0.00%	5.00%	0.00%	5.00%	30.00%
Unknown	100.00%	0.00%	0.00%	0.00%	0.00%	0.00%	0.00%

Table 3.3.1 If you use Lexis+, rate the usefulness to you of the following features: Shephard's Enhanced Analytics.

	No Answer	Essential	Highly Useful	Often Useful	Sometimes Useful	Not really Useful	Not really familiar with this feature
Entire sample	61.19%	1.49%	2.99%	2.99%	2.99%	2.24%	26.12%

Table 3.3.2 If you use Lexis+, rate the usefulness to you of the following features: Shephard's Enhanced Analytics. Broken out by law school enrollment

Law school enrollment	No Answer	Essential	Highly Useful	Often Useful	Sometimes Useful	Not really Useful	Not really familiar with this feature
Less than 400	71.88%	0.00%	0.00%	0.00%	6.25%	3.13%	18.75%
400+ - 550	59.38%	3.13%	6.25%	9.38%	0.00%	3.13%	18.75%
550+ - 800	52.94%	2.94%	5.88%	2.94%	2.94%	0.00%	32.35%
More than 800	61.11%	0.00%	0.00%	0.00%	2.78%	2.78%	33.33%

Table 3.3.3 If you use Lexis+, rate the usefulness to you of the following features: Shephard's Enhanced Analytics. Broken out by academic title

Academic title	No Answer	Essential	Highly Useful	Often Useful	Sometimes Useful	Not really Useful	Not really familiar with this feature
Professor	73.77%	0.00%	0.00%	1.64%	3.28%	0.00%	21.31%
Assistant/ Associate Professor	33.33%	4.76%	9.52%	4.76%	4.76%	0.00%	42.86%
Adjunct/ Clinical Faculty	57.14%	3.57%	3.57%	0.00%	3.57%	7.14%	25.00%
Emeritus	60.00%	0.00%	6.67%	6.67%	0.00%	0.00%	26.67%
Other	55.56%	0.00%	0.00%	11.11%	0.00%	11.11%	22.22%

Table 3.3.4 If you use Lexis+, rate the usefulness to you of the following features: Shephard's Enhanced Analytics. Broken out by age of respondent

Age of respondent	No Answer	Essential	Highly Useful	Often Useful	Sometimes Useful	Not really Useful	Not really familiar with this feature
Under 40	33.33%	0.00%	0.00%	16.67%	16.67%	0.00%	33.33%
40-49	68.42%	5.26%	5.26%	0.00%	0.00%	0.00%	21.05%
50-59	51.52%	3.03%	3.03%	3.03%	9.09%	0.00%	30.30%
60 or over	65.33%	0.00%	2.67%	2.67%	0.00%	4.00%	25.33%
Unknown	100.00%	0.00%	0.00%	0.00%	0.00%	0.00%	0.00%

Table 3.3.5 If you use Lexis+, rate the usefulness to you of the following features: Shephard's Enhanced Analytics. Broken out by gender of respondent

Gender of respondent	No Answer	Essential	Highly Useful	Often Useful	Sometimes Useful	Not really Useful	Not really familiar with this feature
Male	60.00%	0.00%	2.50%	3.75%	1.25%	2.50%	30.00%
Female	60.00%	4.00%	4.00%	2.00%	6.00%	2.00%	22.00%
Other	100.00%	0.00%	0.00%	0.00%	0.00%	0.00%	0.00%

Table 3.3.6 If you use Lexis+, rate the usefulness to you of the following features: Shephard's Enhanced Analytics. Broken out by public or private law school

Public or private law school	No Answer	Essential	Highly Useful	Often Useful	Sometimes Useful	Not really Useful	Not really familiar with this feature
Public	59.26%	2.47%	3.70%	2.47%	4.94%	3.70%	23.46%
Private	64.15%	0.00%	1.89%	3.77%	0.00%	0.00%	30.19%

Table 3.3.7 If you use Lexis+, rate the usefulness to you of the following features: Shephard's Enhanced Analytics. Broken out by # of courses taught last semester

# of courses taught last semester	No Answer	Essential	Highly Useful	Often Useful	Sometimes Useful	Not really Useful	Not really familiar with this feature
None	44.44%	0.00%	7.41%	3.70%	3.70%	3.70%	37.04%
One	67.50%	5.00%	2.50%	2.50%	2.50%	0.00%	20.00%
Two	61.02%	0.00%	1.69%	3.39%	3.39%	3.39%	27.12%
More than two	87.50%	0.00%	0.00%	0.00%	0.00%	0.00%	12.50%

Table 3.3.8 If you use Lexis+, rate the usefulness to you of the following features: Shephard's Enhanced Analytics. Broken out by ranking

Ranking	No Answer	Essential	Highly Useful	Often Useful	Sometimes Useful	Not really Useful	Not really familiar with this feature
Top 20 law school	77.78%	3.70%	0.00%	0.00%	3.70%	0.00%	14.81%
Somewhere in the 21-75 rank	49.09%	1.82%	5.45%	5.45%	0.00%	3.64%	34.55%
76 to 250	60.87%	0.00%	2.17%	2.17%	6.52%	2.17%	26.09%
Other	100.00%	0.00%	0.00%	0.00%	0.00%	0.00%	0.00%

Table 3.3.9 If you use Lexis+, rate the usefulness to you of the following features: Shephard's Enhanced Analytics. Broken out by political views

Political views	No Answer	Essential	Highly Useful	Often Useful	Sometimes Useful	Not really Useful	Not really familiar with this feature
Conservative	71.43%	0.00%	0.00%	0.00%	0.00%	0.00%	28.57%
Centrist	61.76%	0.00%	0.00%	2.94%	5.88%	0.00%	29.41%
Liberal	58.46%	1.54%	0.00%	3.08%	3.08%	4.62%	29.23%
Left of Liberal	60.00%	5.00%	20.00%	5.00%	0.00%	0.00%	10.00%
Unknown	100.00%	0.00%	0.00%	0.00%	0.00%	0.00%	0.00%

Table 3.4.1 If you use Lexis+, rate the usefulness to you of the following features: Research Map.

	No Answer	Essential	Highly Useful	Often Useful	Sometimes Useful	Not really Useful	Not really familiar with this feature
Entire sample	61.94%	0.75%	1.49%	0.00%	3.73%	0.00%	32.09%

Table 3.4.2 If you use Lexis+, rate the usefulness to you of the following features: Research Map. Broken out by law school enrollment

Law school enrollment	No Answer	Essential	Highly Useful	Often Useful	Sometimes Useful	Not really Useful	Not really familiar with this feature
Less than 400	71.88%	0.00%	0.00%	0.00%	0.00%	0.00%	28.13%
400+ - 550	59.38%	0.00%	3.13%	0.00%	9.38%	0.00%	28.13%
550+ - 800	55.88%	2.94%	0.00%	0.00%	2.94%	0.00%	38.24%
More than 800	61.11%	0.00%	2.78%	0.00%	2.78%	0.00%	33.33%

Table 3.4.3 If you use Lexis+, rate the usefulness to you of the following features: Research Map. Broken out by academic title

Academic title	No Answer	Essential	Highly Useful	Often Useful	Sometimes Useful	Not really Useful	Not really familiar with this feature
Professor	73.77%	0.00%	1.64%	0.00%	0.00%	0.00%	24.59%
Assistant/ Associate Professor	33.33%	0.00%	4.76%	0.00%	14.29%	0.00%	47.62%
Adjunct/ Clinical Faculty	57.14%	3.57%	0.00%	0.00%	7.14%	0.00%	32.14%
Emeritus	66.67%	0.00%	0.00%	0.00%	0.00%	0.00%	33.33%
Other	55.56%	0.00%	0.00%	0.00%	0.00%	0.00%	44.44%

Table 3.4.4 If you use Lexis+, rate the usefulness to you of the following features: Research Map. Broken out by age of respondent

Age of respondent	No Answer	Essential	Highly Useful	Often Useful	Sometimes Useful	Not really Useful	Not really familiar with this feature
Under 40	33.33%	0.00%	0.00%	0.00%	33.33%	0.00%	33.33%
40-49	68.42%	0.00%	5.26%	0.00%	5.26%	0.00%	21.05%
50-59	51.52%	3.03%	3.03%	0.00%	3.03%	0.00%	39.39%
60 or over	66.67%	0.00%	0.00%	0.00%	1.33%	0.00%	32.00%
Unknown	100.00%	0.00%	0.00%	0.00%	0.00%	0.00%	0.00%

Table 3.4.5 If you use Lexis+, rate the usefulness to you of the following features: Research Map. Broken out by gender of respondent

Gender of respondent	No Answer	Essential	Highly Useful	Often Useful	Sometimes Useful	Not really Useful	Not really familiar with this feature
Male	61.25%	0.00%	0.00%	0.00%	1.25%	0.00%	37.50%
Female	60.00%	2.00%	4.00%	0.00%	8.00%	0.00%	26.00%
Other	100.00%	0.00%	0.00%	0.00%	0.00%	0.00%	0.00%

Table 3.4.6 If you use Lexis+, rate the usefulness to you of the following features: Research Map. Broken out by public or private law school

Public or private law school	No Answer	Essential	Highly Useful	Often Useful	Sometimes Useful	Not really Useful	Not really familiar with this feature
Public	59.26%	1.23%	1.23%	0.00%	6.17%	0.00%	32.10%
Private	66.04%	0.00%	1.89%	0.00%	0.00%	0.00%	32.08%

Table 3.4.7 If you use Lexis+, rate the usefulness to you of the following features: Research Map. Broken out by # of courses taught last semester

# of courses taught last semester	No Answer	Essential	Highly Useful	Often Useful	Sometimes Useful	Not really Useful	Not really familiar with this feature
None	48.15%	0.00%	0.00%	0.00%	3.70%	0.00%	48.15%
One	67.50%	2.50%	5.00%	0.00%	5.00%	0.00%	20.00%
Two	61.02%	0.00%	0.00%	0.00%	3.39%	0.00%	35.59%
More than two	87.50%	0.00%	0.00%	0.00%	0.00%	0.00%	12.50%

Table 3.4.8 If you use Lexis+, rate the usefulness to you of the following features: Research Map. Broken out by ranking

Ranking	No Answer	Essential	Highly Useful	Often Useful	Sometimes Useful	Not really Useful	Not really familiar with this feature
Top 20 law school	77.78%	3.70%	0.00%	0.00%	3.70%	0.00%	14.81%
Somewhere in the 21-75 rank	50.91%	0.00%	3.64%	0.00%	3.64%	0.00%	41.82%
76 to 250	60.87%	0.00%	0.00%	0.00%	4.35%	0.00%	34.78%
Other	100.00%	0.00%	0.00%	0.00%	0.00%	0.00%	0.00%

Table 3.4.9 If you use Lexis+, rate the usefulness to you of the following features: Research Map. Broken out by political views

Political views	No Answer	Essential	Highly Useful	Often Useful	Sometimes Useful	Not really Useful	Not really familiar with this feature
Conservative	71.43%	0.00%	0.00%	0.00%	0.00%	0.00%	28.57%
Centrist	64.71%	0.00%	0.00%	0.00%	2.94%	0.00%	32.35%
Liberal	58.46%	1.54%	1.54%	0.00%	4.62%	0.00%	33.85%
Left of Liberal	60.00%	0.00%	5.00%	0.00%	5.00%	0.00%	30.00%
Unknown	100.00%	0.00%	0.00%	0.00%	0.00%	0.00%	0.00%

Table 3.5.1 If you use Lexis+, rate the usefulness to you of the following features: Content Recommendations.

	No Answer	Essential	Highly Useful	Often Useful	Sometimes Useful	Not really Useful	Not really familiar with this feature
Entire sample	61.94%	0.00%	1.49%	1.49%	3.73%	1.49%	29.85%

Table 3.5.2 If you use Lexis+, rate the usefulness to you of the following features: Content Recommendations. Broken out by law school enrollment

Law school enrollment	No Answer	Essential	Highly Useful	Often Useful	Sometimes Useful	Not really Useful	Not really familiar with this feature
Less than 400	71.88%	0.00%	0.00%	0.00%	3.13%	3.13%	21.88%
400+ - 550	59.38%	0.00%	3.13%	3.13%	3.13%	3.13%	28.13%
550+ - 800	55.88%	0.00%	0.00%	2.94%	5.88%	0.00%	35.29%
More than 800	61.11%	0.00%	2.78%	0.00%	2.78%	0.00%	33.33%

Table 3.5.3 If you use Lexis+, rate the usefulness to you of the following features: Content Recommendations. Broken out by academic title

Academic title	No Answer	Essential	Highly Useful	Often Useful	Sometimes Useful	Not really Useful	Not really familiar with this feature
Professor	73.77%	0.00%	1.64%	0.00%	0.00%	0.00%	24.59%
Assistant/ Associate Professor	33.33%	0.00%	4.76%	4.76%	9.52%	4.76%	42.86%
Adjunct/ Clinical Faculty	57.14%	0.00%	0.00%	3.57%	7.14%	3.57%	28.57%
Emeritus	66.67%	0.00%	0.00%	0.00%	0.00%	0.00%	33.33%
Other	55.56%	0.00%	0.00%	0.00%	11.11%	0.00%	33.33%

Table 3.5.4 If you use Lexis+, rate the usefulness to you of the following features: Content Recommendations. Broken out by age of respondent

Age of respondent	No Answer	Essential	Highly Useful	Often Useful	Sometimes Useful	Not really Useful	Not really familiar with this feature
Under 40	33.33%	0.00%	0.00%	16.67%	16.67%	0.00%	33.33%
40-49	68.42%	0.00%	5.26%	0.00%	5.26%	0.00%	21.05%
50-59	51.52%	0.00%	3.03%	3.03%	3.03%	3.03%	36.36%
60 or over	66.67%	0.00%	0.00%	0.00%	2.67%	1.33%	29.33%
Unknown	100.00%	0.00%	0.00%	0.00%	0.00%	0.00%	0.00%

Table 3.5.5 If you use Lexis+, rate the usefulness to you of the following features: Content Recommendations. Broken out by gender of respondent

Gender of respondent	No Answer	Essential	Highly Useful	Often Useful	Sometimes Useful	Not really Useful	Not really familiar with this feature
Male	61.25%	0.00%	0.00%	0.00%	1.25%	2.50%	35.00%
Female	60.00%	0.00%	4.00%	4.00%	8.00%	0.00%	24.00%
Other	100.00%	0.00%	0.00%	0.00%	0.00%	0.00%	0.00%

Table 3.5.6 If you use Lexis+, rate the usefulness to you of the following features: Content Recommendations. Broken out by public or private law school

Public or private law school	No Answer	Essential	Highly Useful	Often Useful	Sometimes Useful	Not really Useful	Not really familiar with this feature
Public	59.26%	0.00%	1.23%	2.47%	6.17%	1.23%	29.63%
Private	66.04%	0.00%	1.89%	0.00%	0.00%	1.89%	30.19%

Table 3.5.7 If you use Lexis+, rate the usefulness to you of the following features: Content Recommendations. Broken out by # of courses taught last semester

# of courses taught last semester	No Answer	Essential	Highly Useful	Often Useful	Sometimes Useful	Not really Useful	Not really familiar with this feature
None	48.15%	0.00%	0.00%	0.00%	7.41%	0.00%	44.44%
One	67.50%	0.00%	5.00%	2.50%	5.00%	0.00%	20.00%
Two	61.02%	0.00%	0.00%	1.69%	1.69%	3.39%	32.20%
More than two	87.50%	0.00%	0.00%	0.00%	0.00%	0.00%	12.50%

Table 3.5.8 If you use Lexis+, rate the usefulness to you of the following features: Content Recommendations. Broken out by ranking

Ranking	No Answer	Essential	Highly Useful	Often Useful	Sometimes Useful	Not really Useful	Not really familiar with this feature
Top 20 law school	77.78%	0.00%	0.00%	3.70%	3.70%	0.00%	14.81%
Somewhere in the 21-75 rank	50.91%	0.00%	3.64%	0.00%	3.64%	1.82%	40.00%
76 to 250	60.87%	0.00%	0.00%	2.17%	4.35%	2.17%	30.43%
Other	100.00%	0.00%	0.00%	0.00%	0.00%	0.00%	0.00%

Table 3.5.9 If you use Lexis+, rate the usefulness to you of the following features: Content Recommendations. Broken out by political views

Political views	No Answer	Essential	Highly Useful	Often Useful	Sometimes Useful	Not really Useful	Not really familiar with this feature
Conservative	71.43%	0.00%	0.00%	0.00%	0.00%	0.00%	28.57%
Centrist	64.71%	0.00%	0.00%	0.00%	2.94%	2.94%	29.41%
Liberal	58.46%	0.00%	1.54%	3.08%	3.08%	1.54%	32.31%
Left of Liberal	60.00%	0.00%	5.00%	0.00%	10.00%	0.00%	25.00%
Unknown	100.00%	0.00%	0.00%	0.00%	0.00%	0.00%	0.00%

Table 3.6.1 If you use Lexis+, rate the usefulness to you of the following features: Brief Analyzer.

	No Answer	Essential	Highly Useful	Often Useful	Sometimes Useful	Not really Useful	Not really familiar with this feature
Entire sample	61.19%	0.00%	1.49%	1.49%	2.24%	1.49%	32.09%

Table 3.6.2 If you use Lexis+, rate the usefulness to you of the following features: Brief Analyzer. Broken out by law school enrollment

Law school enrollment	No Answer	Essential	Highly Useful	Often Useful	Sometimes Useful	Not really Useful	Not really familiar with this feature
Less than 400	68.75%	0.00%	3.13%	0.00%	0.00%	0.00%	28.13%
400+ - 550	59.38%	0.00%	0.00%	0.00%	3.13%	6.25%	31.25%
550+ - 800	55.88%	0.00%	0.00%	2.94%	2.94%	0.00%	38.24%
More than 800	61.11%	0.00%	2.78%	2.78%	2.78%	0.00%	30.56%

Table 3.6.3 If you use Lexis+, rate the usefulness to you of the following features: Brief Analyzer. Broken out by academic title

Academic title	No Answer	Essential	Highly Useful	Often Useful	Sometimes Useful	Not really Useful	Not really familiar with this feature
Professor	72.13%	0.00%	3.28%	0.00%	0.00%	0.00%	24.59%
Assistant/ Associate Professor	33.33%	0.00%	0.00%	0.00%	9.52%	4.76%	52.38%
Adjunct/ Clinical Faculty	57.14%	0.00%	0.00%	7.14%	3.57%	3.57%	28.57%
Emeritus	66.67%	0.00%	0.00%	0.00%	0.00%	0.00%	33.33%
Other	55.56%	0.00%	0.00%	0.00%	0.00%	0.00%	44.44%

Table 3.6.4 If you use Lexis+, rate the usefulness to you of the following features: Brief Analyzer. Broken out by age of respondent

Age of respondent	No Answer	Essential	Highly Useful	Often Useful	Sometimes Useful	Not really Useful	Not really familiar with this feature
Under 40	33.33%	0.00%	0.00%	0.00%	16.67%	0.00%	50.00%
40-49	68.42%	0.00%	5.26%	0.00%	0.00%	5.26%	21.05%
50-59	51.52%	0.00%	0.00%	3.03%	6.06%	0.00%	39.39%
60 or over	65.33%	0.00%	1.33%	1.33%	0.00%	1.33%	30.67%
Unknown	100.00%	0.00%	0.00%	0.00%	0.00%	0.00%	0.00%

Table 3.6.5 If you use Lexis+, rate the usefulness to you of the following features: Brief Analyzer. Broken out by gender of respondent

Gender of respondent	No Answer	Essential	Highly Useful	Often Useful	Sometimes Useful	Not really Useful	Not really familiar with this feature
Male	60.00%	0.00%	1.25%	1.25%	0.00%	1.25%	36.25%
Female	60.00%	0.00%	2.00%	2.00%	6.00%	2.00%	28.00%
Other	100.00%	0.00%	0.00%	0.00%	0.00%	0.00%	0.00%

Table 3.6.6 If you use Lexis+, rate the usefulness to you of the following features: Brief Analyzer. Broken out by public or private law school

Public or private law school	No Answer	Essential	Highly Useful	Often Useful	Sometimes Useful	Not really Useful	Not really familiar with this feature
Public	59.26%	0.00%	0.00%	2.47%	3.70%	2.47%	32.10%
Private	64.15%	0.00%	3.77%	0.00%	0.00%	0.00%	32.08%

Table 3.6.7 If you use Lexis+, rate the usefulness to you of the following features: Brief Analyzer. Broken out by # of courses taught last semester

# of courses taught last semester	No Answer	Essential	Highly Useful	Often Useful	Sometimes Useful	Not really Useful	Not really familiar with this feature
None	48.15%	0.00%	0.00%	3.70%	3.70%	0.00%	44.44%
One	67.50%	0.00%	2.50%	2.50%	5.00%	2.50%	20.00%
Two	59.32%	0.00%	1.69%	0.00%	0.00%	1.69%	37.29%
More than two	87.50%	0.00%	0.00%	0.00%	0.00%	0.00%	12.50%

Table 3.6.8 If you use Lexis+, rate the usefulness to you of the following features: Brief Analyzer. Broken out by ranking

Ranking	No Answer	Essential	Highly Useful	Often Useful	Sometimes Useful	Not really Useful	Not really familiar with this feature
Top 20 law school	77.78%	0.00%	0.00%	3.70%	3.70%	0.00%	14.81%
Somewhere in the 21-75 rank	50.91%	0.00%	1.82%	1.82%	1.82%	3.64%	40.00%
76 to 250	58.70%	0.00%	2.17%	0.00%	2.17%	0.00%	36.96%
Other	100.00%	0.00%	0.00%	0.00%	0.00%	0.00%	0.00%

Table 3.6.9 If you use Lexis+, rate the usefulness to you of the following features: Brief Analyzer. Broken out by political views

Political views	No Answer	Essential	Highly Useful	Often Useful	Sometimes Useful	Not really Useful	Not really familiar with this feature
Conservative	71.43%	0.00%	0.00%	0.00%	0.00%	0.00%	28.57%
Centrist	64.71%	0.00%	0.00%	0.00%	2.94%	0.00%	32.35%
Liberal	56.92%	0.00%	3.08%	3.08%	1.54%	1.54%	33.85%
Left of Liberal	60.00%	0.00%	0.00%	0.00%	5.00%	5.00%	30.00%
Unknown	100.00%	0.00%	0.00%	0.00%	0.00%	0.00%	0.00%

Table 3.7.1 If you use Lexis+, rate the usefulness to you of the following features: Contract Review.

	No Answer	Essential	Highly Useful	Often Useful	Sometimes Useful	Not really Useful	Not really familiar with this feature
Entire sample	61.94%	0.00%	0.75%	0.00%	2.24%	2.24%	32.84%

Table 3.7.2 If you use Lexis+, rate the usefulness to you of the following features: Contract Review. Broken out by law school enrollment

Law school enrollment	No Answer	Essential	Highly Useful	Often Useful	Sometimes Useful	Not really Useful	Not really familiar with this feature
Less than 400	68.75%	0.00%	3.13%	0.00%	3.13%	0.00%	25.00%
400+ - 550	59.38%	0.00%	0.00%	0.00%	0.00%	6.25%	34.38%
550+ - 800	58.82%	0.00%	0.00%	0.00%	2.94%	0.00%	38.24%
More than 800	61.11%	0.00%	0.00%	0.00%	2.78%	2.78%	33.33%

Table 3.7.3 If you use Lexis+, rate the usefulness to you of the following features: Contract Review. Broken out by academic title

Academic title	No Answer	Essential	Highly Useful	Often Useful	Sometimes Useful	Not really Useful	Not really familiar with this feature
Professor	72.13%	0.00%	1.64%	0.00%	0.00%	0.00%	26.23%
Assistant/ Associate Professor	33.33%	0.00%	0.00%	0.00%	4.76%	4.76%	57.14%
Adjunct/ Clinical Faculty	57.14%	0.00%	0.00%	0.00%	3.57%	7.14%	32.14%
Emeritus	73.33%	0.00%	0.00%	0.00%	0.00%	0.00%	26.67%
Other	55.56%	0.00%	0.00%	0.00%	11.11%	0.00%	33.33%

Table 3.7.4 If you use Lexis+, rate the usefulness to you of the following features: Contract Review. Broken out by age of respondent

Age of respondent	No Answer	Essential	Highly Useful	Often Useful	Sometimes Useful	Not really Useful	Not really familiar with this feature
Under 40	33.33%	0.00%	0.00%	0.00%	16.67%	0.00%	50.00%
40-49	68.42%	0.00%	0.00%	0.00%	0.00%	5.26%	26.32%
50-59	51.52%	0.00%	0.00%	0.00%	3.03%	0.00%	45.45%
60 or over	66.67%	0.00%	1.33%	0.00%	1.33%	2.67%	28.00%
Unknown	100.00%	0.00%	0.00%	0.00%	0.00%	0.00%	0.00%

Table 3.7.5 If you use Lexis+, rate the usefulness to you of the following features: Contract Review. Broken out by gender of respondent

Gender of respondent	No Answer	Essential	Highly Useful	Often Useful	Sometimes Useful	Not really Useful	Not really familiar with this feature
Male	60.00%	0.00%	1.25%	0.00%	0.00%	2.50%	36.25%
Female	62.00%	0.00%	0.00%	0.00%	6.00%	2.00%	30.00%
Other	100.00%	0.00%	0.00%	0.00%	0.00%	0.00%	0.00%

Table 3.7.6 If you use Lexis+, rate the usefulness to you of the following features: Contract Review. Broken out by public or private law school

Public or private law school	No Answer	Essential	Highly Useful	Often Useful	Sometimes Useful	Not really Useful	Not really familiar with this feature
Public	60.49%	0.00%	0.00%	0.00%	3.70%	3.70%	32.10%
Private	64.15%	0.00%	1.89%	0.00%	0.00%	0.00%	33.96%

Table 3.7.7 If you use Lexis+, rate the usefulness to you of the following features: Contract Review. Broken out by # of courses taught last semester

# of courses taught last semester	No Answer	Essential	Highly Useful	Often Useful	Sometimes Useful	Not really Useful	Not really familiar with this feature
None	51.85%	0.00%	0.00%	0.00%	3.70%	3.70%	40.74%
One	67.50%	0.00%	0.00%	0.00%	2.50%	2.50%	27.50%
Two	59.32%	0.00%	1.69%	0.00%	1.69%	1.69%	35.59%
More than two	87.50%	0.00%	0.00%	0.00%	0.00%	0.00%	12.50%

Table 3.7.8 If you use Lexis+, rate the usefulness to you of the following features: Contract Review. Broken out by ranking

Ranking	No Answer	Essential	Highly Useful	Often Useful	Sometimes Useful	Not really Useful	Not really familiar with this feature
Top 20 law school	77.78%	0.00%	0.00%	0.00%	3.70%	0.00%	18.52%
Somewhere in the 21-75 rank	50.91%	0.00%	0.00%	0.00%	0.00%	5.45%	43.64%
76 to 250	60.87%	0.00%	2.17%	0.00%	4.35%	0.00%	32.61%
Other	100.00%	0.00%	0.00%	0.00%	0.00%	0.00%	0.00%

Table 3.7.9 If you use Lexis+, rate the usefulness to you of the following features: Contract Review. Broken out by political views

Political views	No Answer	Essential	Highly Useful	Often Useful	Sometimes Useful	Not really Useful	Not really familiar with this feature
Conservative	71.43%	0.00%	0.00%	0.00%	0.00%	0.00%	28.57%
Centrist	64.71%	0.00%	0.00%	0.00%	2.94%	0.00%	32.35%
Liberal	58.46%	0.00%	1.54%	0.00%	3.08%	3.08%	33.85%
Left of Liberal	60.00%	0.00%	0.00%	0.00%	0.00%	5.00%	35.00%
Unknown	100.00%	0.00%	0.00%	0.00%	0.00%	0.00%	0.00%

Table 4.1 How important do you feel that it is to equip law students with the skills to use the newest emerging artificial intelligence powered legal research tools of legal publishers and information services?

	No Answer	Extremely important	Very important	Somewhat important	Not so important	Not at all important
Entire sample	8.96%	29.10%	34.33%	23.13%	3.73%	0.75%

Table 4.2 How important do you feel it is to equip law students with the skills to use the newest emerging artificial intelligence powered legal research tools of legal publishers and information services? Broken out by law school enrollment

Law school enrollment	No Answer	Extremely important	Very important	Somewhat important	Not so important	Not at all important
Less than 400	12.50%	28.13%	40.63%	15.63%	3.13%	0.00%
400+ - 550	15.63%	37.50%	25.00%	18.75%	3.13%	0.00%
550+ - 800	2.94%	32.35%	32.35%	26.47%	5.88%	0.00%
More than 800	5.56%	19.44%	38.89%	30.56%	2.78%	2.78%

Table 4.3 How important do you feel it is to equip law students with the skills to use the newest emerging artificial intelligence powered legal research tools of legal publishers and information services? Broken out by academic title

Academic title	No Answer	Extremely important	Very important	Somewhat important	Not so important	Not at all important
Professor	9.84%	26.23%	36.07%	24.59%	1.64%	1.64%
Assistant/ Associate Professor	4.76%	28.57%	23.81%	38.10%	4.76%	0.00%
Adjunct/ Clinical Faculty	10.71%	39.29%	35.71%	7.14%	7.14%	0.00%
Emeritus	6.67%	13.33%	40.00%	33.33%	6.67%	0.00%
Other	11.11%	44.44%	33.33%	11.11%	0.00%	0.00%

Table 4.4 How important do you feel it is to equip law students with the skills to use the newest emerging artificial intelligence powered legal research tools of legal publishers and information services? Broken out by age of respondent

Age of respondent	No Answer	Extremely important	Very important	Somewhat important	Not so important	Not at all important
Under 40	0.00%	50.00%	16.67%	33.33%	0.00%	0.00%
40-49	15.79%	42.11%	15.79%	21.05%	5.26%	0.00%
50-59	3.03%	27.27%	42.42%	24.24%	3.03%	0.00%
60 or over	10.67%	25.33%	37.33%	21.33%	4.00%	1.33%
Unknown	0.00%	0.00%	0.00%	100.00%	0.00%	0.00%

Table 4.5 How important do you feel it is to equip law students with the skills to use the newest emerging artificial intelligence powered legal research tools of legal publishers and information services? Broken out by gender of respondent

Gender of respondent	No Answer	Extremely important	Very important	Somewhat important	Not so important	Not at all important
Male	12.50%	22.50%	37.50%	21.25%	5.00%	1.25%
Female	4.00%	36.00%	32.00%	26.00%	2.00%	0.00%
Other	0.00%	75.00%	0.00%	25.00%	0.00%	0.00%

Table 4.6 How important do you feel it is to equip law students with the skills to use the newest emerging artificial intelligence powered legal research tools of legal publishers and information services? Broken out by public or private law school

Public or private law school	No Answer	Extremely important	Very important	Somewhat important	Not so important	Not at all important
Public	9.88%	29.63%	33.33%	22.22%	4.94%	0.00%
Private	7.55%	28.30%	35.85%	24.53%	1.89%	1.89%

Table 4.7 How important do you feel it is to equip law students with the skills to use the newest emerging artificial intelligence powered legal research tools of legal publishers and information services? Broken out by # of courses taught last semester

# of courses taught last semester	No Answer	Extremely important	Very important	Somewhat important	Not so important	Not at all important
None	3.70%	29.63%	33.33%	25.93%	3.70%	3.70%
One	2.50%	27.50%	45.00%	20.00%	5.00%	0.00%
Two	11.86%	28.81%	32.20%	23.73%	3.39%	0.00%
More than two	37.50%	37.50%	0.00%	25.00%	0.00%	0.00%

Table 4.8 How important do you feel that it is to equip law students with the skills to use the newest emerging artificial intelligence powered legal research tools of legal publishers and information services? Broken out by ranking

Ranking	No Answer	Extremely important	Very important	Somewhat important	Not so important	Not at all important
Top 20 law school	14.81%	25.93%	25.93%	25.93%	3.70%	3.70%
Somewhere in the 21-75 rank	5.45%	36.36%	32.73%	20.00%	5.45%	0.00%
76 to 250	6.52%	21.74%	41.30%	28.26%	2.17%	0.00%
Other	33.33%	33.33%	33.33%	0.00%	0.00%	0.00%

Table 4.9 How important do you feel that it is to equip law students with the skills to use the newest emerging artificial intelligence powered legal research tools of legal publishers and information services? Broken out by political views

Political views	No Answer	Extremely important	Very important	Somewhat important	Not so important	Not at all important
Conservative	7.14%	35.71%	28.57%	14.29%	7.14%	7.14%
Centrist	17.65%	20.59%	26.47%	32.35%	2.94%	0.00%
Liberal	6.15%	32.31%	40.00%	20.00%	1.54%	0.00%
Left of Liberal	5.00%	30.00%	30.00%	25.00%	10.00%	0.00%
Unknown	0.00%	0.00%	100.00%	0.00%	0.00%	0.00%

Table 5.1 How helpful has your law school library been in explaining how to use these new tools?

	No Answer	Extremely helpful	Very helpful	Somewhat helpful	Not so helpful	Not at all helpful
Entire sample	15.67%	16.42%	23.13%	25.37%	11.19%	8.21%

Table 5.2 How helpful has your law school library been in explaining how to use these new tools? Broken out by law school enrollment

Law school enrollment	No Answer	Extremely helpful	Very helpful	Somewhat helpful	Not so helpful	Not at all helpful
Less than 400	25.00%	15.63%	25.00%	15.63%	15.63%	3.13%
400+ - 550	12.50%	18.75%	21.88%	28.13%	12.50%	6.25%
550+ - 800	8.82%	17.65%	32.35%	29.41%	2.94%	8.82%
More than 800	16.67%	13.89%	13.89%	27.78%	13.89%	13.89%

Table 5.3 How helpful has your law school library been in explaining how to use these new tools? Broken out by academic title

Academic title	No Answer	Extremely helpful	Very helpful	Somewhat helpful	Not so helpful	Not at all helpful
Professor	13.11%	9.84%	22.95%	29.51%	13.11%	11.48%
Assistant/ Associate Professor	4.76%	23.81%	38.10%	23.81%	9.52%	0.00%
Adjunct/ Clinical Faculty	25.00%	17.86%	14.29%	17.86%	10.71%	14.29%
Emeritus	26.67%	6.67%	20.00%	33.33%	13.33%	0.00%
Other	11.11%	55.56%	22.22%	11.11%	0.00%	0.00%

Table 5.4 How helpful has your law school library been in explaining how to use these new tools? Broken out by age of respondent

Age of respondent	No Answer	Extremely helpful	Very helpful	Somewhat helpful	Not so helpful	Not at all helpful
Under 40	0.00%	16.67%	50.00%	16.67%	16.67%	0.00%
40-49	31.58%	21.05%	10.53%	26.32%	5.26%	5.26%
50-59	9.09%	21.21%	27.27%	15.15%	18.18%	9.09%
60 or over	16.00%	13.33%	22.67%	29.33%	9.33%	9.33%
Unknown	0.00%	0.00%	0.00%	100.00%	0.00%	0.00%

Table 5.5 How helpful has your law school library been in explaining how to use these new tools? Broken out by gender of respondent

Gender of respondent	No Answer	Extremely helpful	Very helpful	Somewhat helpful	Not so helpful	Not at all helpful
Male	18.75%	12.50%	21.25%	27.50%	11.25%	8.75%
Female	10.00%	24.00%	28.00%	20.00%	12.00%	6.00%
Other	25.00%	0.00%	0.00%	50.00%	0.00%	25.00%

Table 5.6 How helpful has your law school library been in explaining how to use these new tools? Broken out by public or private law school

Public or private law school	No Answer	Extremely helpful	Very helpful	Somewhat helpful	Not so helpful	Not at all helpful
Public	17.28%	19.75%	25.93%	24.69%	9.88%	2.47%
Private	13.21%	11.32%	18.87%	26.42%	13.21%	16.98%

Table 5.7 How helpful has your law school library been in explaining how to use these new tools? Broken out by # of courses taught last semester

# of courses taught last semester	No Answer	Extremely helpful	Very helpful	Somewhat helpful	Not so helpful	Not at all helpful
None	18.52%	14.81%	33.33%	18.52%	7.41%	7.41%
One	7.50%	22.50%	15.00%	35.00%	15.00%	5.00%
Two	13.56%	15.25%	27.12%	22.03%	11.86%	10.17%
More than two	62.50%	0.00%	0.00%	25.00%	0.00%	12.50%

Table 5.8 How helpful has your law school library been in explaining how to use these new tools? Broken out by ranking

Ranking	No Answer	Extremely helpful	Very helpful	Somewhat helpful	Not so helpful	Not at all helpful
Top 20 law school	29.63%	14.81%	7.41%	33.33%	7.41%	7.41%
Somewhere in the 21-75 rank	10.91%	21.82%	25.45%	21.82%	7.27%	12.73%
76 to 250	6.52%	13.04%	32.61%	26.09%	17.39%	4.35%
Other	66.67%	0.00%	0.00%	16.67%	16.67%	0.00%

Table 5.9 How helpful has your law school library been in explaining how to use these new tools? Broken out by political views

Political views	No Answer	Extremely helpful	Very helpful	Somewhat helpful	Not so helpful	Not at all helpful
Conservative	14.29%	14.29%	14.29%	28.57%	14.29%	14.29%
Centrist	26.47%	14.71%	14.71%	29.41%	8.82%	5.88%
Liberal	12.31%	16.92%	30.77%	16.92%	13.85%	9.23%
Left of Liberal	10.00%	20.00%	20.00%	40.00%	5.00%	5.00%
Unknown	0.00%	0.00%	0.00%	100.00%	0.00%	0.00%

www.ingramcontent.com/pod-product-compliance
Lightning Source LLC
LaVergne TN
LVHW082354200926
848481LV00012B/3562
9798885172929